the GODEY
LADY DOLL

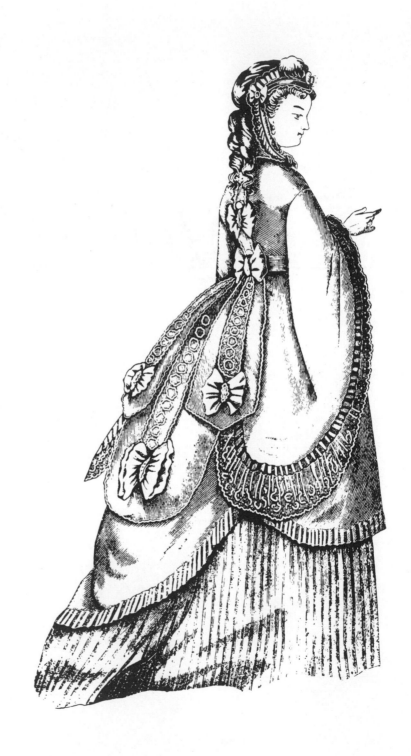

the GODEY LADY DOLL

CHARLOTTE ELDRIDGE

THE STORY OF HER CREATION WITH PATTERNS
FOR DRESSES AND DOLL FURNITURE

HASTINGS HOUSE PUBLISHERS NEW YORK

0-517-110679

COPYRIGHT, MCMLIII, BY CHARLOTTE ELDRIDGE.

ALL RIGHTS RESERVED.

Printed in the United States of America
THE MURRAY PRINTING COMPANY

Library of Congress Catalog Card No.: 53-11685.

c   d   e   f   g   h

To my mother and father, Suzanne and James Blakley, without whose help, encouragement and inspiration this *Godey Lady Doll Book* would not have been possible, and to my favorite dolls, Stephanie and Alice Eldridge.

ACKNOWLEDGMENTS

To the many people who have helped directly and indirectly with the "Godey Lady Doll," the author wishes to express gratitude and appreciation.

Raymond Carlson, Editor, *Arizona Highways* magazine; Alice Hughes, *King Features Syndicate* columnist; Dr. James Rodabaugh, Research Associate and Editor, Ohio State Archeological and Historical Society; Theodore Johnson, President, Walter H. Baker Play Co.; Harry C. Eldridge, Jr., President, Eldridge Publishing Co.; Mrs. Delos Crary for loan of Victorian gown; Hazel Phillips, Curator, "Glendower," Warren County Museum; Mrs. Harry C. Eldridge, Sr.; Bea Alexander, Madame Alexander Doll Co.; Photographers: Karl of Scottsdale, Arizona; Albert Martin, Scottsdale, Arizona; H. H. Welsh, Phoenix, Arizona; The Dayton Art Institute, Dayton, Ohio; Dayton, Ohio, *Journal-Herald;* WLW-T, Cincinnati, Ohio, and women's clubs all over the country.

CONTENTS

ACKNOWLEDGMENTS vii

INTRODUCTION 1

Chapter

1 21
2 27
3 32
4 37
5 40
6 45

THE GODEY LADY DOLL 51

GODEY LADY DOLL DRESS PATTERNS 55
    Basic Patterns 57
    Body Patterns 60-61

PLATE ONE
    Crinoline Underskirt A, Pantalettes, Breasts
    Young Girl's Boots 62-63

PLATE TWO
    Bustle, Crinoline Underskirt B 64-65

PLATE THREE
    Crinoline Underskirt C, Organdy Underskirt
    Slipper 66-67

CONTENTS

DRESS PATTERNS

Pink and Black Lace Lady 68-71
Skating Lady 72-75
Bridal Costume 76-79
Brown Lady 80-83
Golden Brown Lady 84-87
Lavender Lady 88-91
Rose Lace Lady 92-95
Black and Plaid Lady 96-99
Black and Fuchsia Lady 100-103
Young Girl 104-107
Rose Gold Lady 108-111
Nile Green Lady 112-115
Mammy 116-119
Black and White Striped Lady 120-123
Can Can Dancer 124-127

VICTORIAN FURNITURE PATTERNS

PLATE 1. Rose Back Chair, Chippendale Chair . . . 130-131
PLATE 2. Center Table, Bedside Stand, Seth Thomas Clock . 132-133
PLATE 3. Victorian Rocker, Piano Stool, Andirons, Shelf of Books 134-135
PLATE 4. Hepplewhite Chair, Victorian Chair . . . 136-137
PLATE 5. Spinet Piano 138-139
PLATE 6. Empire Sofa, Mid-Victorian 140-141
PLATE 7. Grandfather's Clock 142-143
PLATE 8. Spinning Wheel 144-145
PLATE 9. American Wing Back Chair, Colonial High Back Wall
    Stand . . . . , . 146-147
PLATE 10. Crystal Chandelier 148-149
PLATE 11. Harp 150-151
PLATE 12. Colonial Cradle 152-153
PLATE 13. Wash Stand 154-155
PLATE 14. American Highboy 1780 156-157
PLATE 15. Secretary, Early American 158-159
PLATE 16. Four-Poster Canopy Bed 160-161
PLATE 17. Living Room Setting 162-163
PLATE 18. Bed Room Setting 164-165
PLATE 19. Music Room Setting 166-167
PLATE 20. Detail of Mantel and Fireplace 168-169
PLATE 21. Details of Cupboard and Wainscoting . . 170-171
PLATE 22. Detail of Door and Window 172-173

DIRECTIONS FOR MAKING GODEY LADY DOLL FURNITURE . 175

INDEX 205

X

LIST OF ILLUSTRATIONS

High Style for Godey's Ladies 3
Godey's Book, Title Page 5
Fashion Plate for 1861 6
Child's Fashion Plate 8
Paris Bonnets 9
Typical Godey's Illustration 10
Details of Waist Fashions 11
Fashion Print, "A Nursery Flower" 12
Three Ladies of the Period, 1861-1869 14
Ladies' Riding Dresses 16
When a Penwiper Becomes a Work of Art 17
Detail of Embroidery Pattern 17
A Sample from the Pen of Sarah Josepha Hale . . . 18
A Suburban Residence 19

LIST OF ILLUSTRATIONS

Fashions from Godey's, 1855 23
Further Costumes 24
The Godey Bride 25
Fashionable Ladies 26
The Author with Some of her Early Dolls 29
Victorian Headdress 30
A Page from Godey's Showing Bonnets and Headdresses . . . 31
The Frances Jennings Certificate 34
"Leading Lady of the Month" 35
James Blakley, the Author's Father 42
The Author and her Mother, Susan Blakley 43
Settings Used in Jenny's Department Store 44
Manoreld 47
The Little Mermaid 48
The Little Mermaid as Mortal 49
Virgin Mary and Christ Child Dolls 50
Room Setting Showing Victorian Rocking Chair, etc. . . . 179
Old Colonial Living Room Setting 195
Detail of a Period Living Room 199
Detail of Bedroom Setting 201
Bedroom Setting Showing Colonial Bed 201

INTRODUCTION

IN the early part of the nineteenth century, the status of women in America was little more than that of beribboned and beruffled chattels of their men. Husbands had complete jurisdiction over wives. Fathers had complete authority over daughters. We have little information as to what control bewhiskered gentlemen had over their girl friends, but doubtless it too was complete, since women accomplished little more than delicate Victorian twittering, fluffy chit-chat and attendance on large and demanding families amidst constant swooning when assailed with nineteenth century vapors, i.e. probably too tightly laced corsets.

That they had toned down considerably, however, during Queen Victoria's reign, from the rather ribald and raucous women of the eighteenth century when the world was seeing the be-heading of Marie Antoinette and the cavortings of mad George III, is a matter of history. But not until Sarah Josepha Hale lighted the torch of woman's emancipation with her editorship of *Godey's Lady's Book* in 1837 did women begin the ascent to their present-day position of importance.

Godey's Lady's Book was the "Victorian Bible of the Parlor", the "Harper's Bazaar" and "Vogue" fashion magazine of the period. But actually it was started by a man, Louis Antoine Godey, who in 1830 felt in the mental awakening of the female mind, the source of a good income and a popular trend which he determined to exploit to its greatest degree.

Louis Antoine Godey was the son of middle class American parents who were oblivious to his flare for literature, the closest approach to which he first made by selling newspapers and periodicals on the streets of New York. This didn't satisfy him for long, and presently he was working in a printing establishment which he abandoned in favor of starting his own magazine, *The Lady's Book*.

The *Book* was inconsequential under his direction for nine years, and it was only after he secured the services of Sarah Josepha Hale that it began to achieve national importance. Godey's shrewd eyes had been on Mrs. Hale for many years, in fact it was shortly after she started editing the *Lady's Magazine,* first magazine published in America for women, in 1828, that he began his campaign to win her from his rival periodical.

But Sarah Hale resisted his overtures with a tenacious loyalty to the *Lady's Magazine* and refused to be lured away. Small wonder, since it was this publication that had lifted her from the depths of Victorian despair wherein she played the stock role of the penniless widow with five starving children clustered around her voluminous skirts, who was trying to hold her little flock together at all costs.

She had been a "schoolmarm" before her marriage to David Hale, dashing young lawyer, in the little town of Newport, New Hampshire where they lived. As such she had been relegated to the role of spinsterhood at the age of twenty-five, but she startled the townsfolk by taking lawyer Hale to wed. Theirs was an idyllic union. Three children were born in rapid succession and Sarah went into a "decline." As "hasty consumption" was number one killer of young women of that day, she was left in the hot, musty, overcrowded parlor on a sofa, to die. But David Hale, following the impulse of an ardent young lover, carried her into the high crisp mountain air of New Hampshire in his gig, fed her on purple frost grapes, and in six weeks returned to the village with a rosy-faced, radiant wife.

2

Not too many years later, ironically enough, it was Sarah Hale who tried to snatch her husband from death as she, herself, had been; but fate willed a different outcome. David Hale contracted pneumonia suddenly, and before the frantic wife had time to rally her forces, he was dead.

She was left practically without resources, with four young children to support while expecting a fifth!

Years of hardship followed. Rather than rely upon the mercy of relatives or seek the niggardly positions open to women, Sarah Hale, with her indomitable will, determined to fend for herself as best she could. She tried various ways to make money, from an unsuccessful venture in millinery to writing sentimental verse. Her husband's brother Masons gave her some financial help and it was after the publication of her novel, *Northwood* that her fortunes took a better turn.

The book, which was partly autobiographical, was well received and through it she was offered the editorship of the new *Lady's Magazine,* first publication of its kind in America for women. She accepted the offer and moved with her family to Boston to begin the career that was to bring her fame as the "Duchess of Fiction" and arbiter of morals, manners and fashion for forty years of America's history.

Sarah Josepha Hale edited the *Lady's Magazine* for nine years, finally becoming Louis Godey's editor when he bought out this periodical and merged it with his *Lady's Book* in 1837.

*High style for
Godey's ladies*

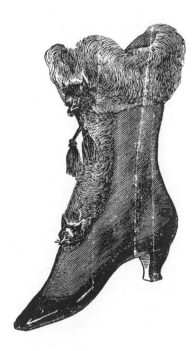

The team of Hale and Godey was to prove an irresistible force in a land which was striving to produce a culture and foster an intellectual awakening among women. Sarah Hale's fire and quiet zeal for the cause of women's education and emancipation put an iron hand on the velvet pen that she guided so shrewdly across the pages of *Godey's Lady's Book.* Early in her career she had cajoled her masculine public cleverly, realizing that their approbation of her magazine was necessary to its success.

"Husbands" she promised, "may rest assured that nothing found on these pages . . . shall cause her [the wife] to be less assiduous in preparing for his reception or cause her to usurp station or encroach on the prerogatives of men. In this age of innovation perhaps no experiment will have an influence more important on the character and happiness of our society than the granting to females the advantages of a systematic and thorough education. The honor of this triumph, in favor of intellect over long established prejudice, belongs to the men of America!" Her flattery was successful. The bewhiskered gentlemen, never sensing the heresy of her words, gave their consent for the fair ladies to read *Godey's,* and thus began the planned campaign that was to help the futile Victorian female find herself, become educated and to continue the mental awakening that has found its blossoming in the twentieth century.

Vassar College as the first school of collegiate rank for women, was aided materially by Sarah Hale and the support of her *Godey's Lady's Book.* As a matter of fact, the original name of "Vassar Female College" was changed by the vehement little editress when she stormed in a letter to Matthew Vassar, founder of the college.

"Female!" she thundered, "what female do you mean? Not a female donkey? Must not your reply be, 'I mean a female woman'? Then . . . why degrade the feminine sex to the level of animals? . . . I write thus earnestly because I wish to have Vassar College take the lead in this great improvement of our language. . . . Pray, do not, my good friend, disappoint me. It is not for myself I expect any benefit. I plead for the good of Vassar College, for the honor of womanhood and the glory of God." [1]

Sensing in the word "female" all the degradation of her sex, she succeeded in her request. The name was changed to Vassar College without the "female", and Sarah Josepha Hale went her crusading way to further liberate the wasp-waisted Victorian woman.

4   [1] Letters, Property of Vassar College.

*Original Title Page
of the Godey's Lady's
Book for 1861*

A typical Godey's fashion plate for 1861 which provided inspiration for the dolls

6

7

She convinced them at least one bath a week was necessary. She pleaded with them to refrain from eating pie for breakfast and always to carry a clean white kerchief; but all of her assorted wheedling, threats and flattery failed to dissuade her Victorian sisters from the injurious waist lacing that was the cause of their many "vapors" and frequent swooning.

She rallied to the cause of women doctors and when Elizabeth Blackwell was having such difficulty entering a medical school, Sarah Hale once more unleashed her genteel but vitriolic pen. It was through her efforts that the medical profession was finally grudgingly opened to the fair sex. She campaigned for public playgrounds for children, better sanitation, better working conditions for women, and child labor laws. She even influenced manufacturers to invent a type of mechanical washing machine to further lift the burden of housekeeping from

THE EVELYN

*Children's style
from Godey's Book*

8

her Victorian sisters' shoulders. On and on burned her crusading fire, always finding an outlet through the aristocratic and proper vehicle of the *Godey's Lady's Book.*

Although one of the first magazines to bring American authors to the fore, authors like Edgar Allen Poe, Harriet Beecher Stowe, Whittier, Horace Greeley, Irving, Longfellow, Holmes, Emerson and Bryant, *Godey's Lady's Book* is perhaps best remembered today for its fashion prints and its sentimental steel engravings which were Louis Antoine Godey's favorites.

He sent his fashion artists to Paris regularly for style inspiration and they attended all the important social functions. He employed the best engravers and printers available and, through the fashion engravings, set the style trend for all America during the period of *Godey's* greatest influence, 1837 to 1877.

Paris inspired bonnets

Fig. 7.—White chip hat, with a very light white feather on one side ; cape trimmed with violet velvet and white blonde strings of white ribbon ; full ruche of white blonde, with a bouquet on the right side.

Illustration used in Godey's, July, 1861, typical of the period

Ever the flamboyant promoter, Godey offered amusing excuses for any error in his beloved magazine. When his "fair readers" complained that often the colors in the fashion prints in their magazine differed from the colors in another copy, he explained it merrily away, saying that this variation was for a very definite reason. "We now colour our plates to different patterns," he wrote in *Godey's* of May, 1839, "so that two persons in a place may compare their fashions and adapt these colours that they suppose may be most suitable to their figures and complexions. . . ."

The real reason for the variation was, however, the fact that women all over the country, employed by *Godey's Magazine* tinted prints in their homes. When these artists ran out of one color they blithely used another, and besides, at such a distance, it was easy to confuse the original color instructions.

But when Louis Godey became too effervescent in his praise of the magazine in January, 1850 by declaring, "*Godey's Lady's Book* will exceed all magazines . . . past, present and to come. . . ." Sarah Hale toned down his exuberant statements and made sure that thenceforth they were more subdued.

Godey's Lady's Book saw a period of American fashion that started in the thirties with billowing skirts, grew ever more elaborate and ponderous with the hoop skirts of the fifties and sixties and finally began a tapering process with the bustle of the seventies which was facetiously called the "bastard" of fashion.

Waists remained waspish throughout the period, but sleeves underwent a definite transition from the leg-of-mutton of the thirties to the skin-tight sleeves of the forties, and so on to the bell sleeve of the fifties.

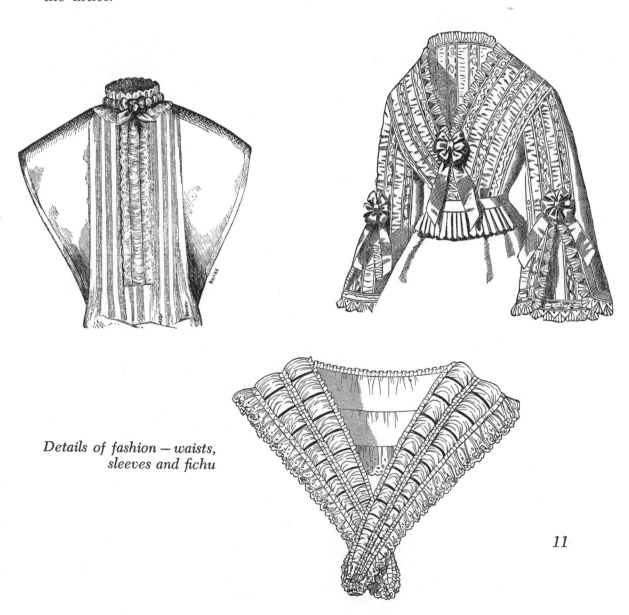

Details of fashion — waists, sleeves and fichu

Typical Godey fashion print,
titled "A Nursery Flower."
From Godey's, April, 1861

12

FASHIONS FOR APRIL 1861.

A NURSERY FLOWER.

Three ladies of the period, 1861-1869
from simplicity to elaborate detail

15

Ladies' riding dresses — Godey's fashions

16

The *Book* not only embraced the vagaries of fashion, but it also influenced the Victorian woman's taste in architecture. House plans were involved and clumsy, interior decoration ran the gamut from fussy antimacassars to minute trivia such as butterfly penwipers and lute pincushions.

When a penwiper becomes a work of art:

The body of the butterfly is of velvet stuffed with cotton and entirely covered with gold beads. The eyes are red and the horns stiff gold cord with a bead on the ends. The wings can be made of cloth or velvet, the latter, however, is much the richest, and two or more colors should be used; they are to be embroidered with silk, fancy beads, and bugles. Pieces of cloth or flannel are cut the same size of the wings and sewed underneath to wipe the pens on. The size of the engraving is the proper size for the penwiper.

A detail of an embroidery pattern

The cookery department lured the nineteenth century female with recipes calling for bird's-nest molds, wine puddings, pickled calves legs and similarly complicated examples of the Victorian cuisine.

Peripatetic Pudding — Six sponge cakes, six eggs, a quarter of a pound of sifted sugar, half a pound of fresh butter, half a pound of marmalade, two glasses of sweet wine. Well mix these ingredients, paper the tin, and bake it about half an hour.

Pikelets — Take three pounds of flour; make a hole in the middle with your hand. Mix two spoonfuls of yeast with a little salt and as much milk as will make the flour into a light paste. Pour the milk with the yeast into the middle of the flour, and stir a little of the flour down into it, then let it stand all night and the next morning work in all the flour; beat it well for a quarter of an hour; let it stand for an hour, take it out with a large spoon, lay it in round cakes on a board well dusted with flour; dredge flour all over them, pat them with your hand, and bake them.

Editorials were long and voluble, stories and serials sentimental with pseudo-romance. But Sarah Josepha Hale's many articles such as the one on making Thanksgiving a national holiday celebrated on one common date throughout the nation, still have a classic ring. She continued to dispense sound psychology and patriotic fervor throughout her tenure as editor of her beloved *Godey's Lady's Book*.

SOME one says that nobody enters a second marriage with the same reverence, or earnestness, or ardor with which he contracted the first. He is older and colder; familiarity with the estate has bred indifference; the being at his side is not a trembling, pure little soul, whom all his strong chivalrous nature rushes forth to protect, but a nice sort of person, who is going to look after his servants, and see that his linen is kept in good order.

A sample from the pen of Sarah Josepha Hale:

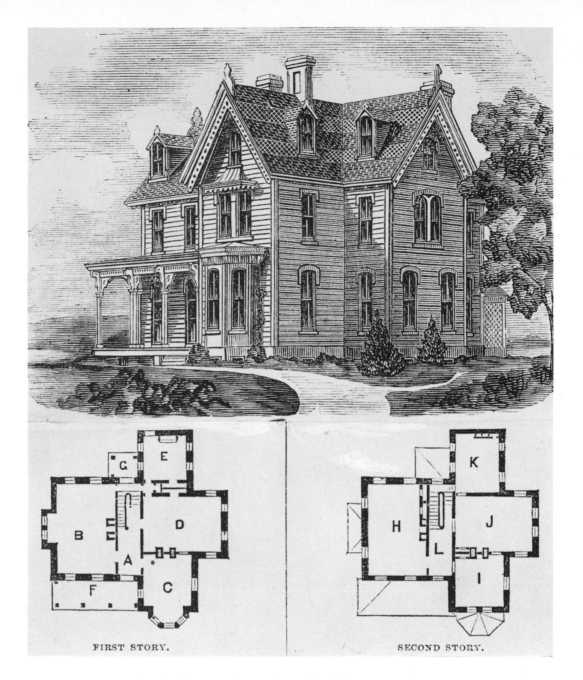

FIRST STORY.　　　　SECOND STORY.

A suburban residence, from Godey's:

The above house, built of frame in very good style, will cost between $3000 and $4000, with marble mantels, heaters, bath, and closets. The design is a plain and ordinary building, simply having those necessary parts common to all houses, so arranged as to give it the appearance of largeness.

First story — A hall, 6′ wide; B parlor, 15′ by 23′9″; C sitting room, 13 by 13′; D dining room 15 by 21′; E kitchen 13′ by 11′9″; F G porches.

Second story — H chamber 15′ by 23′9″; I chamber 13 by 13′; J chamber 15 by 21′; K chamber 13′ to 14′9″; L hall 6′ wide.

The Victorian public looked on in constant amazement that such a handsome monthly magazine as *Godey's* could be published for 25 cents a copy. Besides three or four steel engravings by first-rate artists, the hand colored, double page fashion plate and many black and white woodcuts, the *Book* carried articles of current interest, beauty hints, advice on homemaking, needlework, "Godey's Arm Chair", music and a host of other features. Circulation of 150,000 in a day when that figure was important, made possible the low price of 25 cents per copy.

Louis Antoine Godey's foresight in urging his "fair readers" to have their monthly copies of *Godey's Lady's Book* bound in a leather volume, is the reason we have a few of them preserved today. However, they are increasingly hard to find and thus we consider it a privilege to be able to present this limited resumé of the charming *Godey's Lady's Book*, "Victorian Bible of the Parlor", which has had so considerable an influence even on our present century, and inspired us to create the "Godey Lady Doll."

Charlotte Eldridge

IF anyone had told me in 1941 that in addition to being flat on my back in bed with a stomach ulcer and facing the prospect of having another bald-headed baby daughter, I would also give birth to the "Godey Lady Doll," I would have said that he was completely out of his mind. But that this set of complicated circumstances was to prove a blessing in disguise, I didn't realize until many years later.

When the doctor first relegated me to the bedroom he insisted that I stop writing my newspaper column and any assorted free-lance writing that I had been doing, with strict orders to take it easy. The ulcer was nothing to be treated lightly, as a matter of fact neither were the nauseating pangs of early pregnancy. But to stop my beloved writing was the cruelest blow of all. What could I do with my time?

Since I was allowed a few hours in an easy chair each day or a moment to lounge in the sun in the garden on my *chaise longue*, I soon tired of reading and watching the sky and birds. I could sew. I found restful relaxation in being able to run up a few seams and finally I wheedled the doctor into giving me the privilege of making a simple rag doll for my little four-year old daughter, Stephanie.

Stephanie was a precocious child even at the age of four, and I couldn't see her playing with an ordinary rag-stuffed, saccharine-faced creature. Consequently the first doll turned out to be a sophisticated ten-inch version of a "can can" dancer, complete with black lace stockings, ruffled panties and all. Stephanie was immediately enthralled. So was her mamma. The doll bug had bitten me. There was no returning!

Now I would really make dolls! Let my imagination run wild creating fanciful and beautiful creatures of all types and designs despite ulcer or prospective baby. Needless to say, I kept most of my doll-making activity on a clandestine basis, hiding the evidence under the mattress, behind chairs or in the waste basket, away from prying medical eyes, drawing my mother into the intrigue by forcing her to search the attic and dresser drawers for any scraps and pieces of old lace, silk and trimmings.

First I drew a simple body pattern for a stuffed doll about ten inches in height to be made of flesh-colored silk. (See pattern and directions page 60). This body, filled with kapok, was packed tightly for greater firmness. About a half inch up the leg I creased and sewed to form the little foot. The face was drawn with pencil and then outlined with black embroidery floss, the mouth embroidered in red. Hair was fashioned from yellow- or black- or auburn-colored embroidery floss by stitching it across the top of the head and down the back to give two long strands with which to create the hair-do.

The first costume I dreamed up was of no particular period, but it resulted in an old-fashioned looking lady doll, vaguely of the early Georgian period. Unfortunately none of these original dolls exist today, Stephanie having eventually turned them into wild looking legless characters with her bedtime mauling. However, their first general appearance of quaintness caused the fatal inspiration of using the *Godey's Lady's Book*.

I was enamoured of the little lady dolls as much as Stephanie, partly because at one time in my life I had been a fashion artist and this was just another way to express my love for clothes, except that I wanted the dolls to be more elaborate, more exquisitely costumed,

Inspiring fashions from Godey's, May, 1855

and to possess real features and hands instead of the kapok-stuffed variety. Many hours had I spent in the garden pouring over a few old volumes of *Godey's* when I had nothing better to do. Suddenly one afternoon the idea struck. I will never forget it. I was lying in the shade of my pine trees on the front lawn, sipping cream (my horrible ulcer diet), subconsciously dreaming of all the fantastic doll characters I would create for Stephanie, when the *Godey's Lady's Book* fell open to one of the Victorian fashion plates. I glanced down. Then like a shot I knew what I wanted to do! Create little lady dolls that would look exactly like the old Godey prints! Scanning the pages avidly, I realized it would be no easy task. The costumes were beautiful but elaborate. There were many panniers and bustles and ruffles and tucks and pleats and laces and beads. Too hard! My ulcer would sprout little ulcers if I ever attempted this! But mother — she was visiting me, she was clever with the needle, and had nothing more to do than to see that I stayed quiet and didn't get into too much mischief. Why couldn't mother . . . ?

Late that afternoon found us with my bedroom door locked, secretly cutting out the first Godey costume for the first Godey Lady Doll. We felt like naughty children, and every creak on the stair caused a

Further costumes of the period

GODEY'S FASHIONS FOR NOVEMBER 1861.

24

wild scramble to hide the scissors and silks and Godey fashion prints. But before evening the first costume pattern had come into being with the hardest job of execution yet before us.

It was about three days later that the first Godey Lady was completed, but alas! when Stephanie spied it and was told it was not for her, angry wails engulfed the household. These would be dolls for mamma and her grandmother. They had outgrown little curly-headed girls. The lady was lovely but her face still wasn't satisfactory. I must perfect a method for a sculptured face with real features. I must have real little hands instead of stuffed stubs!

The Godey bride, December, 1874

GODEY'S FASHIONS FOR DECEMBER 1874.

Fashionable ladies, September, 1869

A SECOND little wailing blond was being born about this time and the ulcer was making a graceful exit. Lazy days in the hospital with my new live doll found me dreaming of babies and doll faces and tiny infant hands and tiny doll hands. It was like a superimposed photograph in a television movie. One idea suggested another and it's a wonder I didn't try to stuff Godey prints into Alice's tiny mouth instead of her bottle.

There were busy days to follow with the coming of the new baby, but I managed to get my hands on a lump of plasticine clay to mold a doll face. I shaped it about the size of a small egg, formed a neck and started on the features. My attempt was rewarded with a creature looking like something between Frankenstein's wife and wolf-girl. Leaving young Alice and Stephanie in the care of my colored girl, I hastened to the Art Institute one afternoon. The instructor very kindly put me on the right track. The features took shape, the little face came into being in plasticine clay.

Next we cut one-half inch wedges of sheet tin, sticking them together completely around the head and neck something like a metal halo. (See detailed instructions page 51) I was taught to mix a batch of plaster of Paris and to drop it in layers on the clay face in preparation for making the face mold. When the plaster of Paris had dried, I pried it off and saw the Godey Lady Doll face in reverse. I felt like Michelangelo. After directions from my art teacher, I hurried home to make a *papier mâché* mask.

When my husband found me late that night bending over the kitchen sink, tearing up bits of newspaper into a pan of water when I should have been diapering the new baby, he roared, "Good Lord! What are you doing now"?

"Making a face," I glibly replied. There was no answer. I heard him stomp up the stairs and the bedroom door slam. Small wonder, for I was wrist deep in a mucky mess of wet newspaper and glue which I hoped were the ingredients for a beautiful Godey face. I rinsed out the plaster of Paris mold with water, following instructions, and pressed in about one fourth of an inch of *papier-mâché* all over the inside of the mold. Placing it on the hot-air register in the reception hall to dry, I went to bed in a fever of expectation.

From then on my life was one series of wet newspaper and face molds drying over every hot-air register in the house. The next morning I carefully removed the doll mask from the mold and thus my first doll face was born. Third, I should really say, for the other two were lying upstairs in their cribs.

With a mixture of burnt umber, vermilion and white oil paint, I finally arrived at a flesh tint. Mixing it with a small amount of turpentine (see detailed instructions page 52) I painted the entire face mask. Eyebrows and eyes were painted on in brown with a fine sable brush, the little mouth in red, and a faint touch of pink on the cheeks.

I was excited beyond words. That night baby Alice didn't even get a bottle and my husband's expletives fogged the bathroom mirror.

The next problem was to fasten the doll mask to the body. I found that by stuffing the rag doll head into the mask, I could secure it with carefully placed stitches. The hair went through an evolution of everything from the shavings off home made phonograph records to embroidery floss, yarn and theatrical hair. I even cast my eyes on the children's golden locks but resisted the impulse. I finally settled

The author with some of her early doll creations

on my old stand-by, embroidery floss. The floss extending over the *papier-mâché* forehead was glued on, while the remainder was stitched across the stuffed part of the head and neck. The strands were then twisted into shape, caught with small stitches and formed into a low chignon at the nape of the neck. Curls which had been twined around a toothpick were glued to the forehead as bangs. I even perfected a way to make the popular Victorian neck curls by winding the floss which had been dampened with glue, around one of Stephanie's all-day sucker sticks. The curls were carefully pulled off the stick and tucked under the little wig at the sides of the neck. 29

The doll hands! I still shudder when I think of the series of claws I created in an attempt to perfect a graceful hand. No material was sacred. Even my poor dentist was badgered and bedeviled into giving me a box of dental wax which he used to construct temporary false plates. Using a wire armature of copper wire filched from my husband's workroom, I tried modeling the hands from different materials. The wax was out — so also was a gooey mixture I had concocted from salt, flour and water. I finally learned to make creditable hands many months later when we visited Colorado and the owner of our motel taught me how to make them of ceramic clay. (See instructions page 53).

At last the body-making reached a point which partially satisfied

Victorian headdress of 1861

30

me, but I was still striving for perfection. All this time we were costuming the Godey Ladies in fashions from the old prints of 1842 through 1888. Alice was growing up in the midst of a flutter of Victorian laces and silks, beads and passementerie, blobs of *papier mâché*, glue, embroidery floss and kapok. Stephanie's small hands were ever eagerly awaiting an unguarded moment when she could make short shrift of our worktable and many a fist did I run down small throats digging out beads and sequins and buttons amid loud wails. Mother's nimble fingers were fashioning bustles, crinoline skirts, panniers in miniature while I made lace-bedecked pantalettes, ruffled petticoats, slippers, and drew more designs for future patterns from the Godey Lady fashion prints. Soon we had enough dolls for a small exhibit.

A page from Godey's, showing bonnets and headdresses

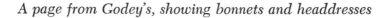

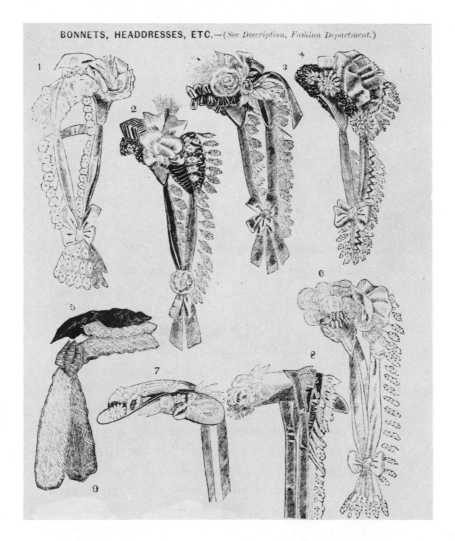

31

OUR friends came and looked at the dolls and "ohed" and "ahed". "Such beautiful creatures"! they said. They fingered the small stitches and examined the laces and beads and tiny jewelry and asked us what we intended to do with them. That was what we were wondering. We loved each little Godey Lady too much to part with any of them. To sell one doll would be like getting rid of the children for twenty-five dollars apiece.

Since the toy buyer of our largest department store was a friend of mine, I carried the Godey Lady Dolls up to him one afternoon in December. There were six, ranging in period from 1855 to 1867. He was delighted but wanted to know if they were for sale.

"No," I replied, "my mother and I made them."

"But if they aren't for sale," he asked, "what are they for?"

"That's what I want you to suggest," I answered.

It was only a few weeks before Christmas and the result of our conversation was an exhibit of the Godey Ladies in the corner toy window. We were as proud as new parents. It was seeing my dream come to life. That this exhibit was to be the beginning of a hobby that would later turn into a business and was so far reaching as to affect the course of my whole life, I could not foresee.

Phone calls and mail followed the showing. Elderly women, young women and children were enchanted by the little ladies. They wanted to know where we had found the authentic Victorian fabrics, how we made the dolls. They wanted to know all about the old *Godey's Lady's Book*. They began asking me to speak to Sunday school classes, women's clubs, church groups and assorted gatherings, to tell how I had been inspired by *Godey's* and how we first executed the dolls with such perfection.

My husband snorted when I gave myself the fancy title of "Fabric Sculptor", a term which I originated but which has since been copied many times. The local newspapers began writing up our activities with photographs of mother and me doing the actual work. By this time our studio (really the library transformed into a sewing room) had outgrown itself. We had twenty dolls, no place to keep them and still no organized plan of action. The house was littered with tiny feathered bonnets, reticules and miniature lace mitts, ruffled pantalettes, jewelry made from seed pearls, crystal brooches torn apart and settings out of old rings. The "little people" had really taken over! Nothing escaped us. We had even cut up one of my husband's favorite ties for a panel down the front of an 1870 bustled gown. That was one of his most unhappy days. I noticed him staring at this particular doll which I was so proudly displaying.

"That dress looks vaguely familiar," he said.

I snatched the doll behind my back and tried to distract his attention. He was livid. Needless to say, whenever I cut up any more of his clothing I always hid the evidence. But his handkerchiefs did make such wonderful Victorian lingerie!

In the meantime I had started writing again and was on the staff of a magazine in New York. The Godey Doll-making was still my hobby and relaxation, but I had taken my great-grandmother's name of Frances Jennings to distinguish my doll-making activities from my writing. Now I was known as "Frances Jennings — Fabric Sculptor — Creator of the Godey Lady Doll". Since my writing for the magazine consisted mostly of articles about the early cavortings of Alice and Stephanie whose pictures in all manner of undress adorned

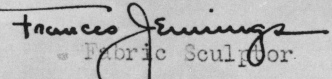

Godey Lady Doll

" Evening dress of pink silk, made
with two skirts trimmed with point
lace. White lace bodice trimmed
with pink silk bretelles and point
lace. Headdress of lace and roses. "
GODEY'S LADY'S BOOK Sept. 1869

Frances Jennings

Fabric Sculptor

**Copyright 1945. Authentic copy from Godey Lady's Book.
Created by Frances Jennings, Franklin, Ohio.**

The Frances Jennings Certificate

the pages, I was called to New York frequently. I determined to take the collection of ladies with me on my next trip east to see what would happen.

In New York my friend Alice Hughes, syndicate columnist, saw them and was charmed. She suggested an outlet that had never occured to me. I hurried over to the imposing Fifth Avenue establishment of W. & J. Sloane. The head decorator had just returned from Europe. He took one look at the Godey Ladies and said, "Can you make six of them for us within a month? We would like to use them under antique bell glasses to be placed in the debutante bedroom in the 'House Of Years'."

I gasped, "Of course. What is your preference of period and color?"

My heart was still racing when I left Sloane's. The Godey Dolls were to sell for one hundred dollars apiece. We would make three hundred dollars! Such a flurry when I arrived home! Even Stephanie

34

*"Leading Lady of the Month," from Today's Woman magazine,
with her daughters, Stephanie and Alice*

and Alice tried to get into the act by pawing through our boxes of lace
and fabrics. We finally pacified them with a few cast-off bodies that
they draped into wild looking caricatures of the Victorian ladies.
After sleepless nights, pricked fingers, tired eyes and weeks of happy
exhaustion, we finally shipped the last doll to Sloane's.

My father, who lived several miles away, was on the verge of
divorcing my mother. My husband was sure we had come to the
parting of the ways. They were two irate males. Mother would come
down to my house, presumably for an afternoon's work on the dolls,
and stay three days. Meal schedules were off. Fortunately the colored
maid was not involved with the sewing and she kept the children on

a fairly level routine. But when the telephone would start ringing and I had a deadline to meet on my writing, and the dolls to finish, that would invariably be the day when Alice would get my lipstick and ruin the bedroom wallpaper and Stephanie would eat a butterfly or some other backyard creature. The Godey Dolls had become a dominating force!

In New York they were an immediate success. They were written up by Cholly Knickerbocker, and photographed, and I was made the "Leading Lady of the Month" in *Today's Woman* magazine. The fan mail poured in and newspapers and magazines all over the country carried feature articles on us and the dolls. Finally one day the post office refused to deliver the mail. There was too much of it. We were simply amazed that a little Victorian doll had aroused such interest.

The most exciting letter came from a Mrs. Ethel Mitchell in Glens Falls, New York. She wanted to send me a box of heirloom laces and material, some of it a hundred years old, that had belonged to her family. The package arrived, a large four-inch deep suit box of the most beautiful things we had ever seen. There were satins and passementerie of irridescent beads, old taffetas in shades muted and gray with age, yards of lace, a Spanish mantilla of black lace fine as a cobweb, ribbons of every description, creamy yellow old batiste and cottons, pompadour lace from Paris made over horsehair, lace mitts, pearl trimmings, Alençon lace from France and yards of black sequin insertion. Deep in the middle of this assortment of treasure she had wrapped an 1843 Godey's Lady's Book, one of the rarest volumes. Mother and I were breathless with delight. Our fabrics for the dolls had been authentically Victorian up to this point but with these lovely things we would be creating museum pieces. Mrs. Mitchell's letter held a note of nostalgic sadness. In repayment for her generous gift we made her an exquisite bride doll from a Godey fashion print of 1869. She wrote later that the Godey Lady was to be for her an omen of good fortune since she had just passed through a trying time with the death of her husband.

4

I WAS receiving requests from women's groups out of the state now, to speak to various gatherings and exhibit the Godey Ladies. For a year I had been studying the old *Godey's Lady's Books* that friends had given me, with another nebulous idea in mind which involved not only the fashions but the whole pattern of the Victorian period and its influence on women of my century. I realized that the *Book* had had a far reaching effect. It had been through Sarah Josepha Hale and her editorship of *Godey's* that women had started the slow climb to education and the many reforms that were only now bearing fruit.

Why not formulate my lecture and exhibit of the dolls into a really informative and inspiring project, in addition to the explanation of a fascinating hobby? The idea caught on. Soon I was lecturing in Victorian costume all over Indiana, Illinois, Pennsylvania, Colorado and Kentucky, exhibiting the dolls and trying to inspire modern women into taking a more active interest in world affairs by telling them of the early struggles of their Victorian counterparts, and thus persuade them to carry further the torch which had been lighted in the 1830's by my ideal, Sarah Josepha Hale, editor of *Godey's Lady's Book*. (See Introduction)

First I told the story of how I happened to create the Godey Doll. Then I launched into a brief history of Godey's Book and Sarah Hale, bringing the talk up to the modern time by encouraging my fellow females to get in there and pitch with their men, suggesting that the world might be helped materially out of its state of war and confusion by a little "mothering" instead of so much "fathering." My slogan was: "Intelligence coupled with heart, makes for real wisdom." I sincerely felt that women of my generation had that to give to our century of trouble. That I inspired many a bridge playing mamma I have no doubt. They used to come up to me starry-eyed and eager to do something about something, and I am quite sure they did. I loved them! They also wanted to learn how to make Victorian dolls. My husband had a similar ambition with regard to me, but I was out of town too much.

It was a gay but strenuous life. Many a little out-of-the-way railroad line would see me clamber aboard with my strange assortment of hat boxes full of dolls, old Victorian trunk (which had been dragged down from the cobwebby attic of my hundred-year-old Ohio farmhouse) and suitcases, for a swing around various towns where I had been booked to speak. The newspaper notices were many and varied. One columnist even called me a witch, in a nice sort of way.

"Romantic souls who moan that the good old days are gone forever," she opined, "and say that life isn't what it used to be, should take a lesson from Charlotte Eldridge. Perhaps our frontiers are gone, maybe we don't fight Indians any more and the covered wagons are all in museums, but we are still pioneering. If, on Halloween night you chanced to glance out across the sky and saw a ghostly trio of feminists go flitting by, they probably were Carrie Chapman Catt, Frances E. Willard and Susan B. Anthony. And right behind them in a shiny airplane . . ." (I'm grateful that she didn't say broomstick) . . . "doubtless would be Charlotte Eldridge.

Mrs. Eldridge's mission in this world is to stir up women. 'Women haven't accomplished as much in this world as they should,' she says earnestly, 'Our pioneer women got freedom for us, saw to it that we had the vote, but what have we done with it'?

"Charlotte Eldridge is press agent No. 1 for Sarah Josepha Hale, who was editor of *Godey's Lady's Book* from 1837 to 1877. She became acquainted with Mrs. Hale when she (Mrs. Eldridge) began her hobby of making Godey Lady Dolls some years ago. Mrs. Hale was one of the foremost feminists of her time and Charlotte Eldridge in studying her life became fired with ambition to go and do likewise.

"She gives talks before all kinds of organizations about her dolls and before she is finished she gets around to her main subject which is encouraging women to take a more active interest in politics and world affairs. Not that she believes in pushing the men aside she is quick to say. Women should take their place beside men in the affairs of the world.

"Everywhere she goes Charlotte Eldridge scatters the seeds of pioneering womanhood like some twentieth century Johnny Apple-seed. 'Susan B. Anthony got us the vote,' she says, 'Now let's do something with it'!

"Once Mrs. Eldridge's pioneering plans almost caused a Man-Who-Came-to-Dinner plot. She was to speak to a woman's club in Illinois. Her hostess, wishing to make everything pleasant for her guest, waxed the stairway until it shone like glass. Then the hostess promptly slipped on the steps and sprained her ankle.

"From her bed she telephoned a friend. 'I've sprained my ankle and can't take Mrs. Eldridge to the meeting. Will you look after her'?

"So the friend dashed up the glassy stairs and sprained her ankle! Then came Charlotte Eldridge. She too ran gaily up the stairs to view the casualties. But here the story has a different twist — she didn't sprain her ankle and she gave her lecture on schedule."

Some of the newspapers approached my project from a different angle. "Dolls designed with an idea — peace"! they said. And they were right, for after World War I and II, I was fired with the hope to see war and trouble stop, never dreaming that my little Godey Lady Dolls would help answer my sincere and ardent prayer.

I T was about this time that another brain storm struck. My family always ducked when that strange gleam came into my eyes, for they never knew where it might lead. Especially my father. He and mother would come down for the week end and between stitches try to catch a glimpse of me. One Sunday afternoon I cornered him. We were all sitting around in the living room making plans for my next trip on a speaking engagement and the Godey Lady Dolls were strung out on the floor before the fireplace.

"I should have a better way to display them," I said. "These poor women where I speak have to rig up tables for me to show the dolls and they aren't displayed to their best advantage." My father was looking at me with narrowed eyes.

"Daddy . . . why couldn't you . . ."? and I stooped down beside the dolls, whipped the fireplace screen around behind them, grabbed a stray piece of wallpaper and hung it on the screen and flew to the children's doll house for a small table.

"I want some miniature doll rooms . . . and Victorian furniture to fit the Godey Ladies."

"Oh, no, you don't," said my father, dodging. "Don't look at me like that. You've involved your mother in this thing. You've got everyone in the country sending you their stray scraps. . . . Keep me out of it! I'll have absolutely no part of it"!

"Oh Lord," my husband was moaning, "not this — again"!

Before he left for home that Sunday night, my Father had made sketches of our first miniature Victorian room and we had made a list of the lumber it would require.

I was confident that he could make the miniature room and furniture, for many years earlier, in fact shortly before I was born, he was nationally known for his miniature window displays. He had created small animated scenes that were the talk of the nation but had given all of this up later to enter the building business.

When the first Victorian parlor took shape (see illustration page 42) he called me. He had also finished two chairs and a miniature copy of my favorite antique rose-back sofa that sat in the living room. He was as excited as mother and I. We hung little pictures on the walls and planned the draperies and carpet as carefully as we would decorate a room of our own. Our heads were whirling with ideas for furniture and future rooms. My poor Father looked dazed but happy. He bought whittling tools and more wood. He gathered in a supply of glue and airplane cement. He collected an assortment of paint and varnish and sandpaper and paper clips and nails, while I ransacked the wallpaper stores for tiny patterned paper and cut up old evening gowns for satin draperies.

At last we made a trip over to a town nearby to visit the Warren County Museum and my good friend, Hazel Phillips, curator. The Warren County Museum was one of the most enchanting restored Victorian houses I had seen and I always felt a nostalgic thrill when I walked into its spacious reception hall and high ceilinged rooms. It had originally been built in 1836 for J. Milton Williams and as a museum was filled with the best and most interesting antiques garnered from civic-minded citizens. Here was a treasure-trove of ideas in furnishings and decorations for our miniature Godey rooms. My father followed me about from room to room where we hurriedly sketched melodeons and sofas, cherry chests, wash stands, four-postered can-

James Blakley, the author's father, with Victorian bedroom setting

opied beds, and chandeliers. Another dream was in the making.

We copied every detail possible and figured and planned what materials we would need to carry them out on a small scale of two inches to the foot. My father had more spring to his step than he had had for many years and mother had to watch that he didn't stay up too late at night working on the little furniture. From his clever fingers started to spring spinning wheels and platform rockers, fireplace and-irons and Seth Thomas clocks, mahogany grandfather clocks and gilded harps for the little drawing room. Everything was inspiring us at once. Father was working now as hard as we were, he had no time to make noises when mother became immersed in the sewing. We were like a flock of children, except that the real children, Alice and Stephanie, couldn't play with the doll rooms, they could only watch their elders. However, they managed to assemble quite an assortment of their own. When anything went wrong with a piece of furniture, they made little clucking sounds of real pleasure as we presented it to them.

The author and her mother, Susan Blakley, with Victorian living room setting

At last three rooms were completed, the little parlor we had made originally, a bedroom (see photographs page 199 and page 201) and a larger, more elaborate drawing room complete with ornate mirror above the fireplace and crystal chandelier. Mother and father were like pleased puppies over that chandelier endeavor, for they had combed every possible ten-cent store for mirrored hair barrettes, tiny crystal beads, earrings and even the inside assembly of a fountain pen with which to make the interior of the chandelier. (See photograph page 148)

The bedroom was a complicated project. Not only did it also contain a fireplace with an antique miniature coal scuttle, but a four-postered canopy bed with a hand-crocheted bedspread that mother worked on for weeks, washstand with a soap dish and washbasin, pitcher and a traditional china pot on the lower shelf. I had been haunting all the antique shops in the vicinity for months, collecting every object of minute dimensions that I could find. Father even made a miniature cradle in that bedroom for the new baby.

43

The drawing room with the Victorian bride and her five sisters was supposed to be the natural prelude to the bedroom scene which was a few years later at the time of the arrival of the first infant. We had created a Mammy doll who bent over the child in tender solicitude (see illustration page 201) while the adoring aunties stood about with baskets of flowers and expressions of prim admiration.

Now we were really in business. The newspapers and magazines had a fine time. They carried articles and pictures headlined: DOLLS OF CHARLOTTE ELDRIDGE GET EVERYONE INTO THE ACT. Only the children remained outside the project. But not for long. Already another idea was sprouting. We were exhibiting the dolls and rooms now, not only at women's clubs and university groups where I was lecturing; the art institutes were also showing them and we had worked out an arrangement whereby department stores displayed them for a price, along with their fashions.

Settings used in Jenny's, Cincinnati, department store window

OTHER exciting developments had also come about. The Warren County Pilgrimage, which was a weekend set aside whereby the general public could visit the historic houses of Ohio, had asked us to throw open our hundred-year-old late Greek revival house, "Manoreld", and to exhibit the miniature Godey Lady Dolls and rooms along with our full-sized antiques.

The children and I were to be gowned in Victorian clothes and to play hostess to the throngs of people who wandered through our high-ceilinged, satin-draped rooms. Everything went beautifully except for Alice! She definitely wanted no part of ruffles and pantalettes and the Victorian period, and after a series of wails and curl pulling and tantrums, she ended up spending the weekend at her grandmother's.

On one of my later trips to New York (I was still writing, but under difficulty) I sold the Godey Ladies on royalty to the Madame Alexander Doll Company who manufactured them and put the Godey Lady Dolls on the market that fall. They were larger than our originals but very charming.

The television stations were asking me for interviews, and we found to our delight that the Godey Ladies and miniature rooms televised very well. As a matter of fact, they looked almost real, and that was what gave me the final brain storm involving the children.

If the dolls televised so well, why couldn't I . . .?

Many nights later saw me creating a different kind of character. It was a mermaid doll. Her tail was made of bead and sequin trimming and in her little arms she held a gilded lyre. I rigged up a background setting, using a marine oil painting that had been done by an aunt of mine many years before, placed the mermaid on an abalone shell that had been given to me, piled more shells around her and sea sponges I had gathered off the Florida beaches, made the foam from pink maline that came from heaven knows where (I think it was part of Alice's bassinet), and stuck in pieces of driftwood I had been saving for just such weird occasions as this.

The setting was part of the beautiful Oscar Wilde story, *The Little Mermaid,* that I would tell to the children. The television show would consist of storytelling to Alice and Stephanie and in their dreams the scenes would come to life in miniature. It was called "Charlotte Eldridge Presents", and the children got their first taste of appearing before the cameras. They took it like little troupers. They would putter into the set in matching Victorian pegnoirs, sit at my side on the sofa with their blond curls bobbing, beg for a story and then fall asleep. In their dreams they would see the miniature settings. We did the wonderful one of the Christ Child at Christmas, and I felt inspired as I worked on the Virgin Mary and Joseph dolls. I created the stable set and made the manger out of branches from our apple tree. The angel on the hillside wore a halo cut from a tin can, but she was lovely, and the same pink maline from Alice's bassinet served as foamy clouds with a sky background that I painted with Stephanie's pastel crayons. Many stories did we do on that first television series: "Grandmother's Portrait", "The Selfish Giant", "Toby Titus and Celeste, the Angel", but the children were fast outgrowing the bedtime story phase. The years were passing with a swiftness that was frightening.

Then my life took a surprising and most unexpected turn. The children and I moved thousands of miles from the scene of that first

Manoreld

47

Godey Lady Doll-making and became involved in a very different kind of life, in the southwest, from the one in the quiet little Ohio village. My hobbyhorse turned into a run-away that has led to many pleasant trails. I do a weekly television show in Arizona about the Indians and the desert and the lore of the still pioneer west — a far cry from the Godey Dolls and miniature rooms and all the attendant phases of Victoriana. My hobbyhorse has turned into a real one that I love and am riding towards a western rainbow that I hope has no end.

The Little Mermaid, television setting

The little mermaid turned into a mortal princess

49

The Virgin Mary and Christ Child dolls

50

THE GODEY LADY DOLL

MODELING THE HEAD

Directions for making face mold: — Take a lump of plasticine clay (which may be purchased at any art supply store) about the size of a large egg (see doll body pattern) and form a small neck (following diagram 1). Sculpture features and if there is difficulty in forming pleasing features, secure the help of someone with modeling experience or an art teacher. When plasticine face is completed, cut pieces of tin in wedge shapes and place together all around head and neck about half way back. (See diagram 2.)

THE PLASTER OF PARIS MOLD

Directions for plaster of Paris mold: — Mix about a teacup full of plaster of Paris in an old pan with enough water to make it the consistency of half-melted ice cream, (work fast for plaster will dry quickly). Drop plaster of Paris onto plasticine face until fully covered to a thickness of about half an inch, letting it run off the sides of tin wedges. Let plaster of Paris remain on plasticine until it is thoroughly dry and hardened and then pry plasticine out of mold. The inside of the plaster of Paris mold is the mold for the *papier-mâché* face.

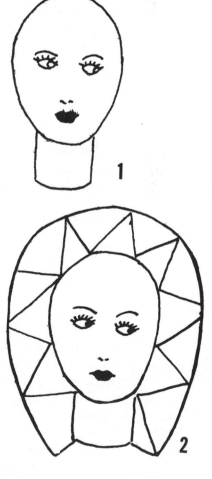

THE PAPIER MACHE FACE

Directions for *papier-mâché* face: — Tear up several sheets of old newspaper rather fine in a pan. Add warm water, enough to dampen paper well and to soak it into a pulp. Let soak over night. By morning it will be in a state where you can pick it up in your hands and squeeze it out and press it into the cavities in the plaster of Paris mold which has been previously rinsed out with water. Press *papier-mâché* into mold to a thickness of about one-fourth inch and let dry. If it can be placed on a hot-air register it will dry more quickly than by room temperature. When *papier-mâché* mask has completely dried, lift it out of mold and paint with a flesh-colored oil paint.

THE GODEY LADY DOLL

PAINTING THE FACE

Directions for painting face: — With artists' oil paints mix a small amount of red and sienna or burnt umber with white oil paint, matching it to the color of human skin. Avoid getting color too pink. Use turpentine for thinner but do not get paint too thin. With a small brush, paint the flesh color on the *papier-mâché* face. When this has dried, sketch with a pencil the eyes and mouth, using a small sable brush for the actual painting. Use burnt umber thinned with a little turpentine for eyes and eyelashes, painting the whites of the eyes with white paint thinned with turpentine. Make a thin mixture of delicate pink for rouge on the cheeks and blend in on face. Paint mouth on in red, the color of your favorite lipstick. You will probably make several of these doll faces before you are satisfied, but continued efforts will be worth the trouble in the completed Godey Lady Doll.

DIRECTIONS FOR MAKING DOLL BODY

MATERIAL: Any kind of soft, flesh-colored silk. Slip material is excellent.

PROCEDURE: Pin doll body pattern to double thickness of silk. Cut out body pattern. Baste two sections together leaving bottom of torso open for stuffing. Sew seams on sewing machine. Stuff kapok or soft cotton into torso and legs, packing in firmly. If desired, run light wire into arms and legs before stuffing. Wire will allow arms and legs to be bent into any position desired. When body is completely stuffed sew up seams that have been left open. Sew legs to body. Bend bottom of leg up about ¾" and catch at side to make foot. Cut about ½" off arm and pull out small amount of stuffing so that ceramic hand can be inserted and glued or sewed onto arm. Face portion of stuffed body can be stuffed into *papier-mâché* mask which is gently sewed into body by catching at the side of the neck.

THE HAIR

Directions for making doll hair: — Hair for the Godey Lady Dolls can be made either from ordinary embroidery floss or theatrical hair which may be purchased at theatrical supply houses in any shade desired. For hairdo made of embroidery floss or theatrical hair, sew sections of hair across stuffed portion of head, gluing hair across *papier-mâché* top of forehead. Catch hair along sides of head where hair would ordinarily stop. Pull hair toward back and twist to form a low chignon on neck. Small curls can be made for forehead by wrapping floss around a toothpick. Dampen floss with glue and let dry. Pull off toothpick and glue curls to forehead. Make side neck curls by twisting floss or hair which has been dampened with glue around an orange stick and let dry. Pull curls off and tuck them under side hairline and catch with invisible stitches. (See Victorian headdress illustration page 30) Decorate hair with small ornaments made of tiny beads, sequins, small flowers, bits of lace, (following Godey fashion print ideas) ribbon, etc. Make small earrings from tiny beads or rhinestones. Necklaces can be made of seed pearls, tiny colored beads, strands of black floss for neck ribbon with medallion of beads or a sequin. Bracelets and rings for hands can be made by the same process of decoration.

THE HANDS

Directions for making doll hands: — The simplest way to have hands for the Godey Lady Doll is to go to a ceramic shop and buy the small hands that are used for the ceramic figurines that are currently so popular. However, doll hands may be made by purchasing ceramic clay (that can be fired) and forming a palm the size of diagram 3. Fingers can be made by rolling pieces of clay until the desired thickness is obtained (see diagram 4) and fastening them to the palm, bending in any desired direction for graceful fingers. Let the hands dry thoroughly and then have them fired at a ceramic shop. Extreme care should be taken of them in this state as they are very fragile until fired. After firing they may be painted with the same shade of oil paint that has been used for the doll face. The tips of the fingers may be touched with a deeper flesh tint to indicate finger nails. The hands may then be either glued to the end of the stuffed arm or bound on with a bit of cloth and sewed firmly. The sleeves of the little Godey costumes will cover this area of the wrist.

The Godey Lady Doll is now ready for the breasts to be sewed on (see Basic Patterns Plate One). Add ballet slippers, pantalettes and petticoats. Costumes may be designed and sewed to doll after all of this preliminary procedure has been completed. Purchase metal doll stand to be placed under skirt to hold doll erect. A tall water glass may be used as substitute for stand.

3

4

GODEY LADY DOLL DRESS PATTERNS

In the following pages are to be found patterns, descriptions and minute instructions covering proper procedure to be observed while fashioning any or all of the fifteen Godey Lady Dolls.

First, select the little lady you desire to duplicate. Have patience to study very carefully the pattern and instructions covering the making and costuming of each individual doll, before starting actual work.

After making body, face, and hands, basic patterns are in order. Make pantalettes, bustle, slippers, crinoline underskirt for stiffening, and last the organdy underskirt.

You are now ready to fashion the costume to adorn the doll of your choice. By all means, do not be discouraged in the search for the specified bits of silk, laces, and ribbons. You will be agreeably surprised at the fun to be experienced in the exploration of trunks and boxes in storage room and attic; and what is more important, if unable to duplicate the various colors and fabrics mentioned in instructions, you can use your own imagination in the selection. The latter will doubtless afford an added thrill, when at last you gaze at the finished creation.

GODEY LADY DOLL BASIC PATTERNS

DIRECTIONS

SUBJECT: Pantalettes
    REFER TO: PLATE ONE — PATTERN PART #1.

MATERIAL NEEDED:
    White Organdy; Narrow white lace for edging.
HOW TO MAKE:
    Seam sides and center. Sew one-fourth inch hem at bottom, and add narrow lace edging. Gather material around ankles and waistline. Sew to doll.

SUBJECT: Organdy Underskirt
    REFER TO: PLATE THREE — PATTERN PART #2.

MATERIAL NEEDED:
    White Organdy; narrow lace edging.
HOW TO MAKE:
    Seam sides; hem bottom, and add gathered or plain lace edging. Gather at waistline, and sew to doll.

SUBJECT: Bustle
    REFER TO: PLATE TWO — PATTERN PART #3.

MATERIAL NEEDED:
    White Organdy; cotton.
HOW TO MAKE:
    Seam around edges; pad with cotton, and sew to doll body at back, waistline.

DESCRIPTIONS

SUBJECT: Slippers
  REFER TO: PLATE THREE — PATTERN PART #4.

MATERIAL NEEDED:
  One-half inch wide black satin ribbon; one-fourth inch wide black satin ribbon for ties.
HOW TO MAKE:
  Fold pattern in two. Leave selvage edges open to insert foot. Center fold is for back of heel. Fold and sew where seam is marked, around to make toe. Make ties from the narrower satin ribbon and fasten at top of heel. Make bow at instep.

SUBJECT: Breasts
  REFER TO: PLATE ONE — PATTERN PART #5.

MATERIAL NEEDED:
  White Organdy; cotton.
HOW TO MAKE:
  Gather material around the edges, leaving sufficient space for padding; after which, draw together, shape properly, and sew to doll body.

SUBJECT: Young Girl's Boots
  REFER TO: PLATE ONE — PATTERN PART #6.

MATERIAL NEEDED:
  Soft black leather or plastic. Black kid glove will do.
HOW TO MAKE:
  Fold pattern at center line. Seam together as marked. Fit properly and sew to foot of doll.

SUBJECT: Crinoline Underskirts.
  REFER TO: PLATE ONE FOR PATTERN PART "A"; PLATE TWO FOR PATTERN PART "B"; PLATE THREE FOR PATTERN PART "C".

MATERIAL NEEDED:
  White crinoline.
HOW TO MAKE:
  Select either the A, B, or C pattern part as mentioned in description covering the costume of each individual doll. Close back seam. Bind bottom with same material which is to be used for making dress skirt.
  Fit around waistline by sewing skirt to doll's body beneath bustle.

BASIC PATTERNS

DRESS PATTERNS

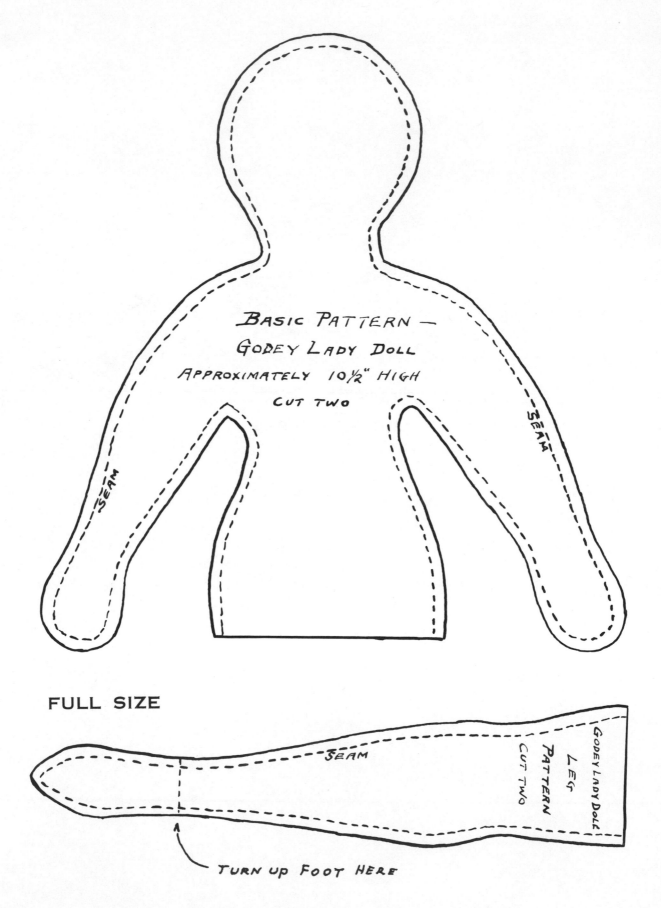

BASIC PATTERN —
GODEY LADY DOLL
APPROXIMATELY 10½" HIGH
CUT TWO

SEAM

SEAM

FULL SIZE

SEAM

GODEY LADY DOLL
LEG
PATTERN
CUT TWO

TURN UP FOOT HERE

GODEY LADY DOLL BODY PATTERN

YOUNG GIRL

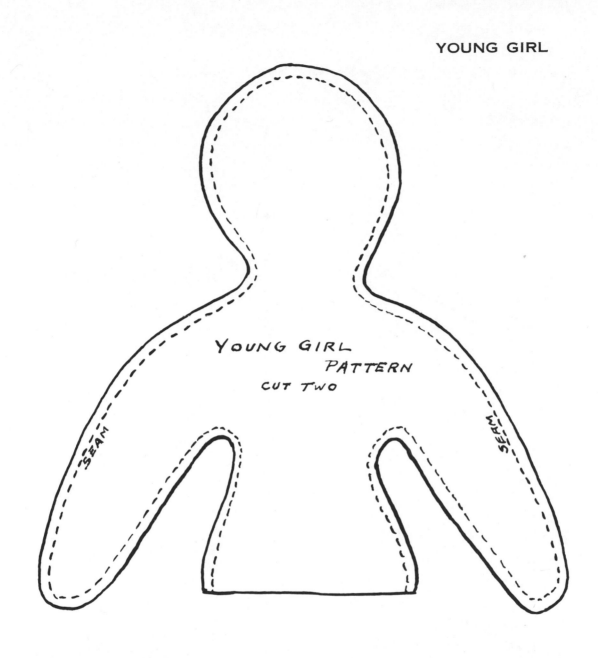

YOUNG GIRL
PATTERN
CUT TWO

SEAM

SEAM

FULL SIZE

SEAM

YOUNG GIRL LEG PATTERN — CUT TWO

TURN UP FOOT HERE

61

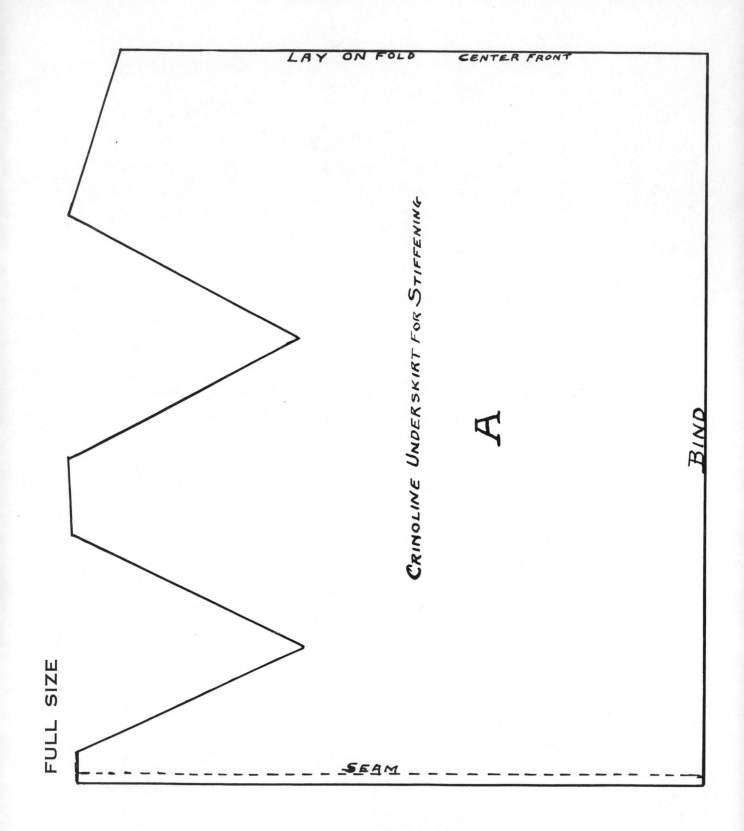

LAY ON FOLD   CENTER FRONT

Crinoline Underskirt For Stiffening

A

BIND

FULL SIZE

SEAM

PLATE ONE

62

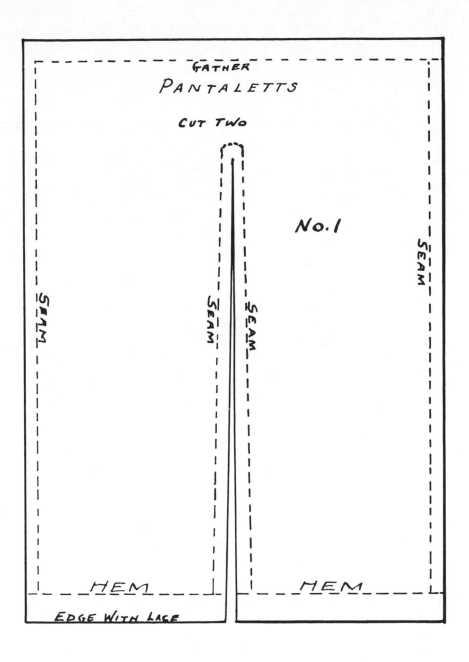

GATHER
PANTALETTS
CUT TWO

No. 1

SEAM

SEAM

SEAM

SEAM

FULL SIZE

HEM

HEM

EDGE WITH LACE

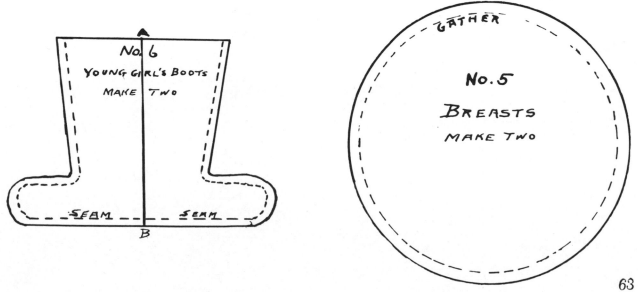

No. 6
YOUNG GIRL'S BOOTS
MAKE TWO

SEAM

SEAM

B

GATHER

No. 5

BREASTS
MAKE TWO

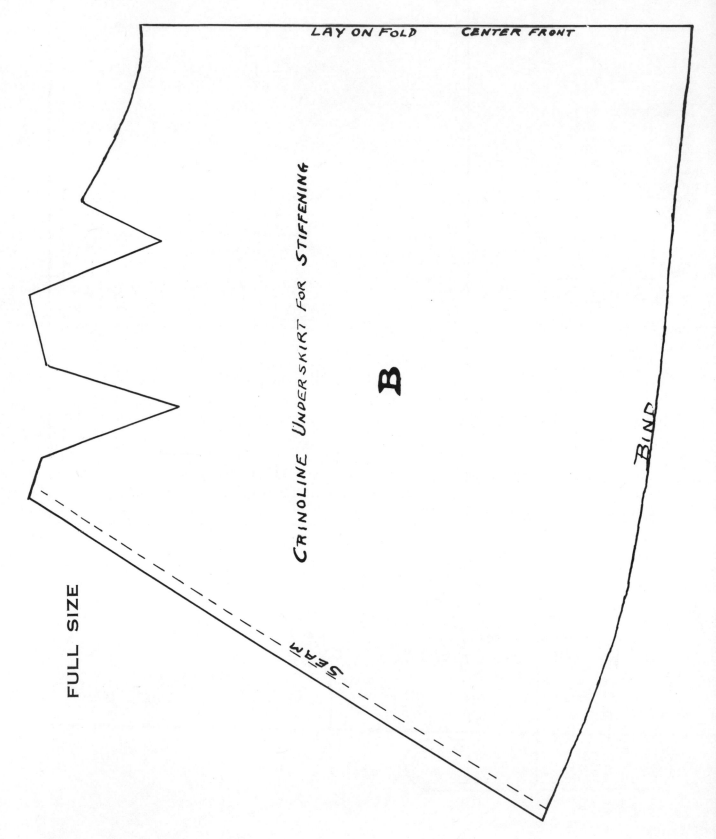

LAY ON FOLD   CENTER FRONT

CRINOLINE UNDERSKIRT FOR STIFFENING

B

BIND

SEAM

FULL SIZE

64

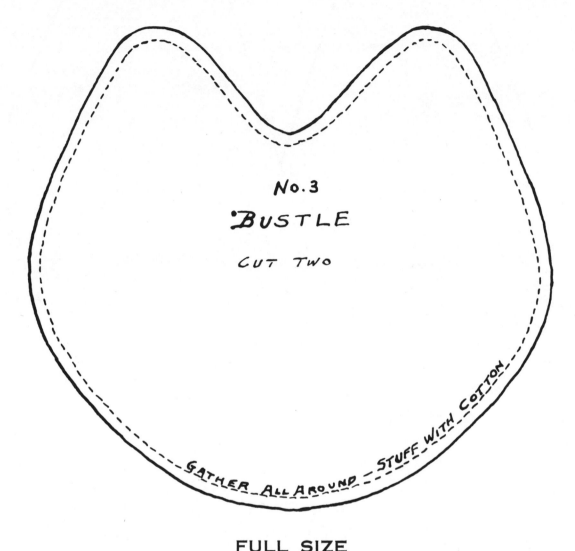

No. 3
BUSTLE
CUT TWO

GATHER ALL AROUND — STUFF WITH COTTON

FULL SIZE

PLATE TWO

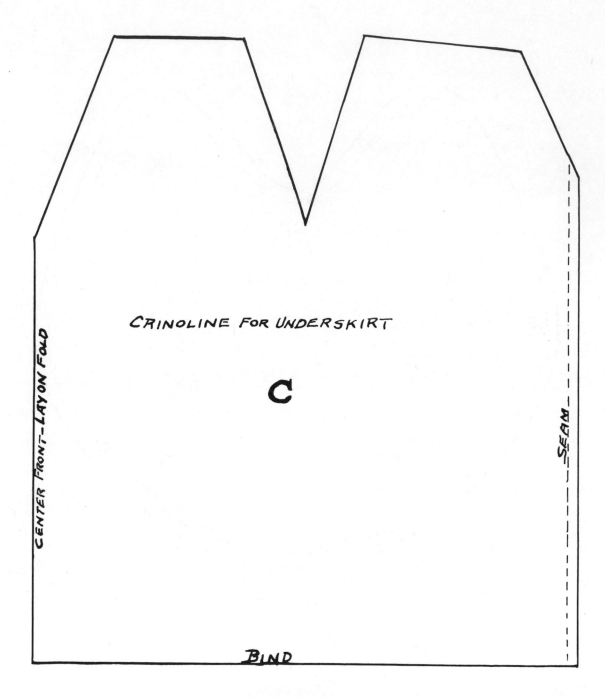

CRINOLINE FOR UNDERSKIRT

C

CENTER FRONT—LAY ON FOLD

SEAM

BIND

FULL SIZE

PLATE THREE

No. 2

ORGANDY UNDERSKIRT

CUT TWO

GATHER AROUND WAIST

SEAM

SEAM

HEM

SEW LACE EDGING AROUND BOTTOM

FULL SIZE

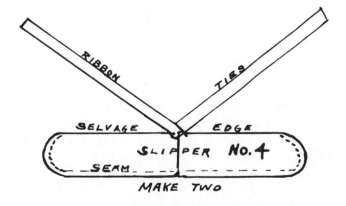

RIBBON

TIES

SELVAGE

EDGE

SLIPPER NO. 4

SEAM

MAKE TWO

PINK AND BLACK LACE LADY — Dinner Dress 1874.

MATERIAL NEEDED:

Salmon-pink velvet; black lace four inches wide; black lace for edging one-fourth inch wide; seed pearls for necklace, earrings, and skirt trimming; black lace for hat; a small cluster of black feathers from an ostrich plume.

HOW TO MAKE:

This doll requires crinoline underskirt "B", as per pattern part shown on Basic Patterns, Plate Two, page 64. Make skirt and sew to doll body according to directions outlined on page 52. The same applies for pantalettes, organdy underskirt, and bustle. Follow carefully instructions for use of dress pattern parts from #1 to #7.

PATTERN PART #1 is for fashioning outside skirt. Cut from salmon-pink velvet. Close back seam. Hem bottom of skirt as indicated. Trim bottom with ¾ inch pink velvet pleating.

Festoon the ¼ inch black lace all around skirt, one inch above pleating with loop each 1½ inches apart, placing seed pearl in each loop. Gather at waistline and sew to doll.

PATTERN PART #2, the front pannier, is made from black silk lace with flower design, using a narrow black silk lace for edging at hem. Gather at waistline and sew to doll body.

PATTERN PART #3, the back pannier, is also made from same material as that specified for front pannier. Gather at top and sew to back, waistline. Narrow lace edging all around.

PATTERN PART #4: This is a crinoline foundation for the six back-pannier puffs.

PATTERN PART #5: These six back-pannier puffs are fashioned from pink velvet. They should be cut on a bias. Gather at sides to stuff. Sew the seams joining the separate puffs together and stuff each puff with a small amount of cotton. Gather each at the top and sew to crinoline foundation in a fan shape. After completion, sew all of them to back waistline on top of black lace pannier already attached to doll.

PATTERN PARTS #6 AND #7: Make bodice and sew to doll. Around the bottom of each sleeve, attach a black lace puff from elbow to wrist. Finish with a narrow band of pink velvet.

Around the waist arrange a belt of pink velvet with flat bow at center back.

HEAD-DRESS: Fashion with black lace crowned with ostrich feathers, and a rosette of pink velvet.

NECKLACE AND EARRINGS: Make from seed pearls similar to those used for trimming dress.

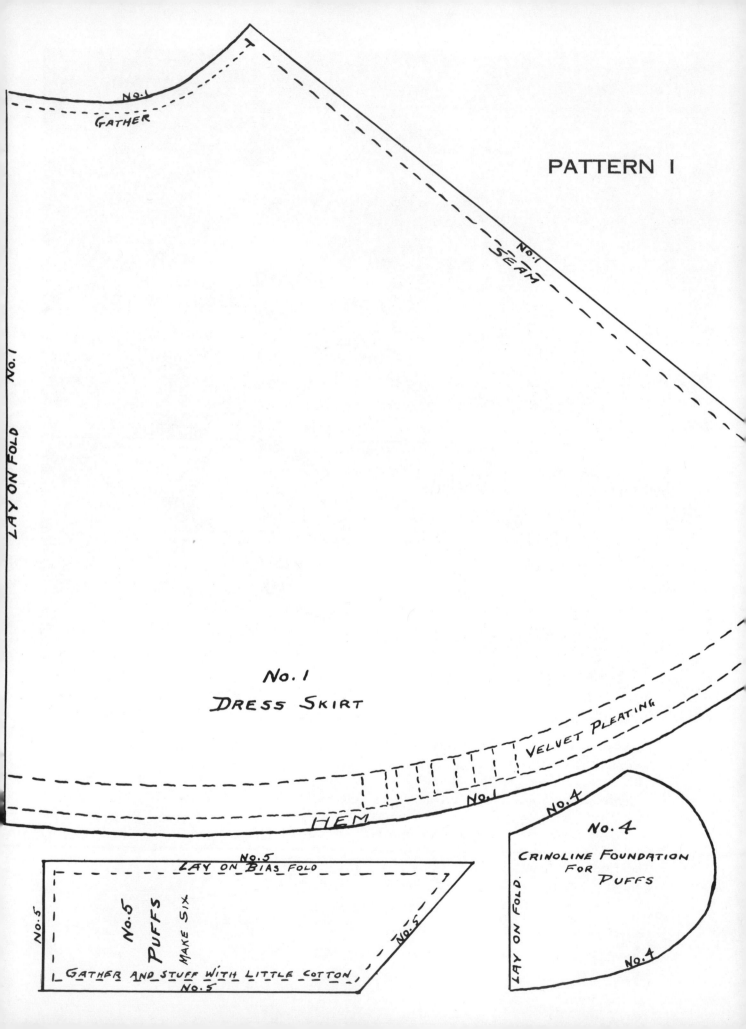

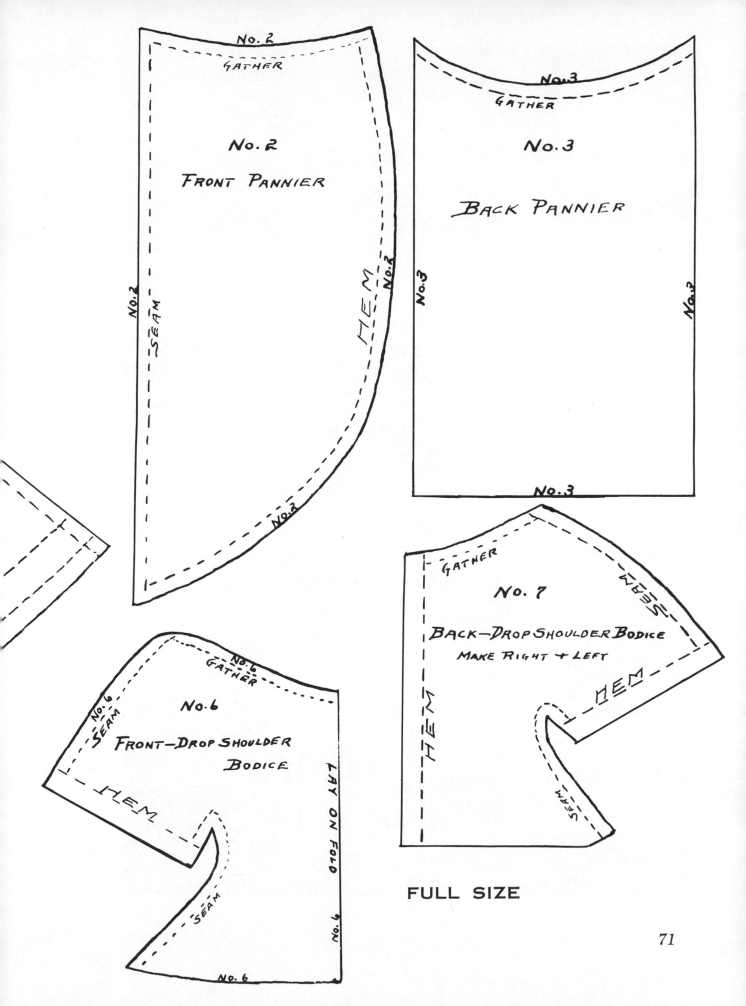

FULL SIZE

71

SKATING LADY — 1859.

MATERIAL NEEDED:

Black and white silk with narrow stripe; black velvet; white fur; black ribbon about ¼ inch wide; a quantity of small jet beads for trimming.

HOW TO MAKE:

This costume requires crinoline underskirt "A", page 64; pantalettes, bustle, etc. After making crinoline underskirt as per directions, add pleated black- and white-striped silk to bottom, three inches in depth.

Now, follow Pattern Parts #1 to #6:

PATTERN PART #1: Make black-and-white-striped silk overskirt, and sew one inch hem at bottom. Then sew to doll's body at waistline. Make three upward pleats each at center front, center back, and on each side about ½ inch above hem (see photo). Suspend from each pleat two one-inch strands of jet beads for trimming.

PATTERN PARTS #2 AND #3: Make jacket of black velvet. Fit to body by closing seams and darts and sew to doll.

PATTERN PARTS #4 AND #5: Fashion both front and back peplums from black velvet edged with white fur. Gather at tops and sew to waistline. Finish with narrow black velvet band.

PATTERN PART #6: Bonnet is made from black velvet, edged with white fur. Close darts; gather back; edge around face and collar with narrow band of white fur and tack to doll.

Make a muff from a small piece of the same white fur. Secure hands inside.

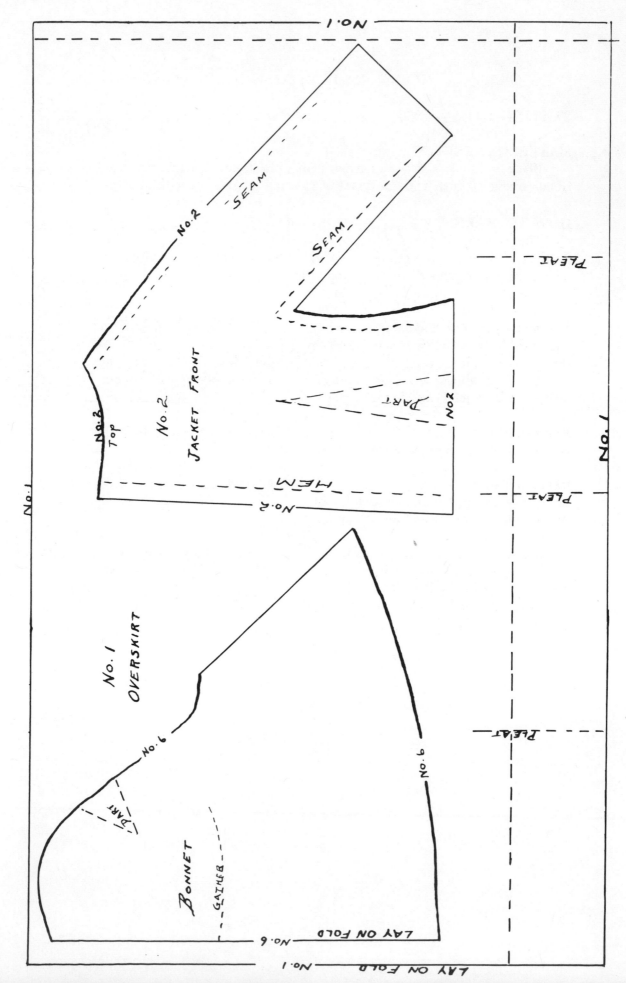

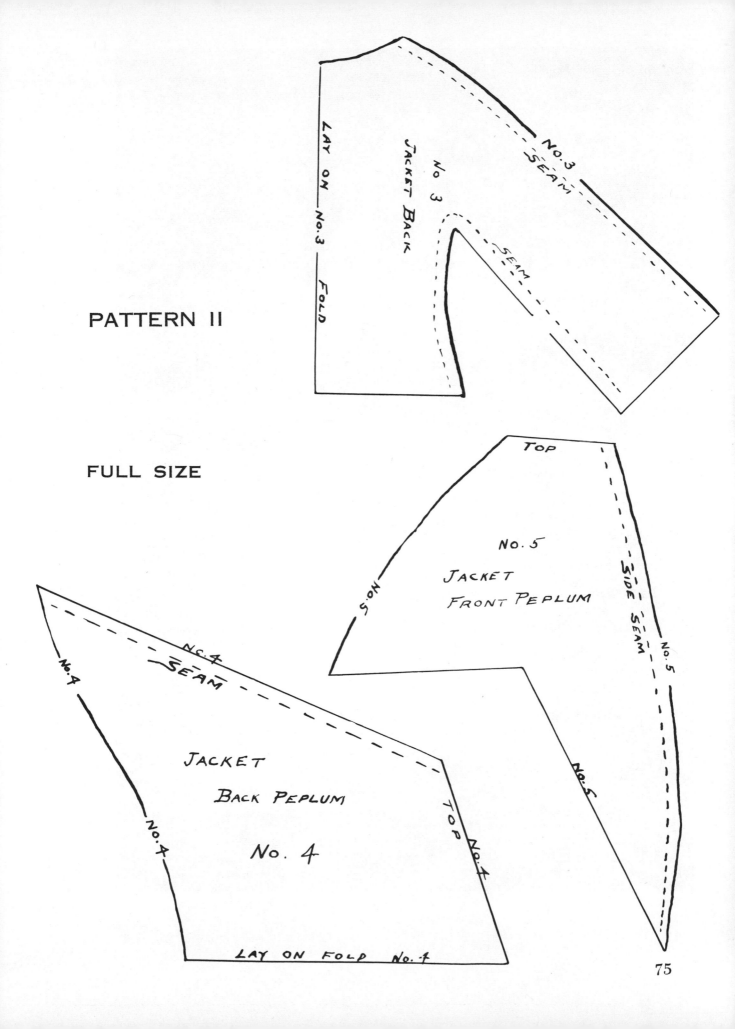

PATTERN II

FULL SIZE

75

BRIDAL COSTUME — 1874.

MATERIAL NEEDED:

   White or egg-shell silk or satin; a portion of elegant lace for front panel of dress; cream-colored net for yoke; narrow lace for edging; one-fourth inch wide satin ribbon; a length of plain net or flowered silk lace for a veil; pearls or brilliants for earrings and brooch.

HOW TO MAKE:

   Make and sew to doll, according to direction on page 52, the basic undergarments, and crinoline underskirt "B" for stiffening. For the latter, consult Plate 2, page 64.

   Follow closely instructions for Pattern Parts #1 to #5.

PATTERN PART #1: Cut outside dress skirt from white or egg-shell silk or satin. Close seams where indicated and sew a one-inch hem at the bottom. Pleat a piece of the dress material 3½ inches wide by 30 inches long. Press and attach to skirt, about 1½ inches from bottom (see photo). Sew a triangular panel of lace five inches long by four inches wide at bottom, to front of skirt. Gather skirt and fasten to doll at waistline.

PATTERN PART #2: Cut yoke from cream colored net. Seam shoulders; pleat with fan-shaped tucks to fit neck; slip over head; sew to doll, and trim neck with gathered lace.

PATTERN PARTS #3, #4, AND #5: These three parts compose the back, front, and sleeves of combination waist and overskirt. Seam shoulders and sides. Gather sleeves top and bottom and sew into combination. Finish at wrist with lace. Hem edges around front and bottom of waist combination and add gathered lace edging. Draw together enough ¼ inch white ribbon to encircle the hem around neck, front, and bottom of waist combination. Attach to waistline in front. Make veil any style to suite taste.

PATTERN III

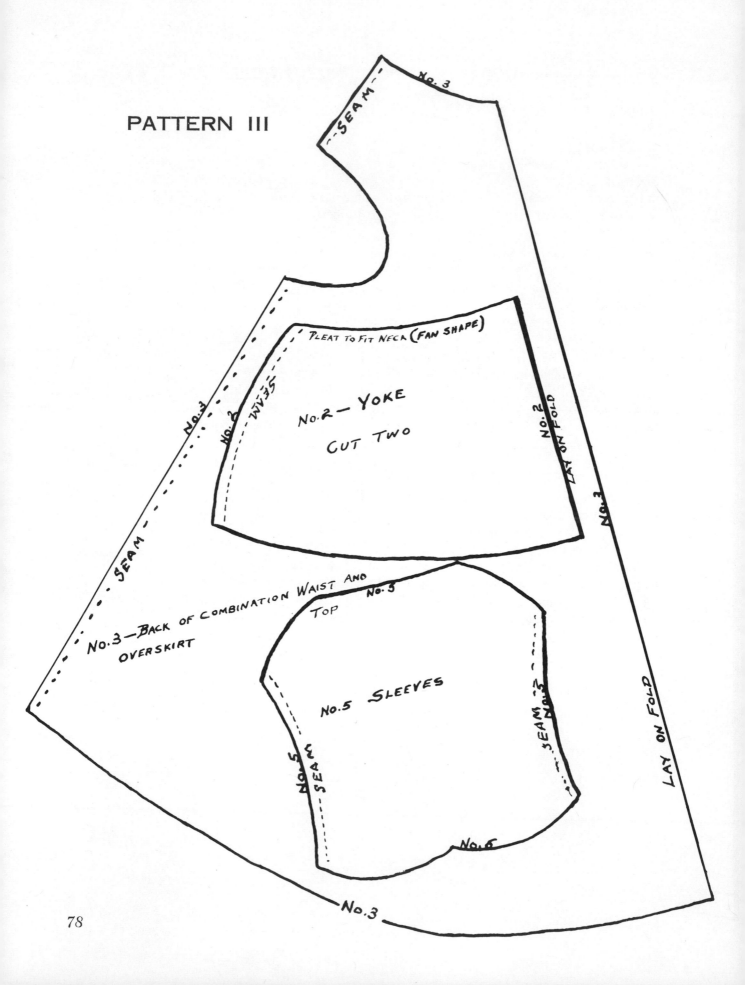

SEAM

No. 3

PLEAT TO FIT NECK (FAN SHAPE)

No. 2 — YOKE

CUT TWO

No. 3

SEAM

No. 2

No. 2

LAY ON FOLD

No. 3

SEAM

No. 3 — BACK OF COMBINATION WAIST AND OVERSKIRT

TOP

No. 5

No. 5 SLEEVES

No. 5

SEAM

SEAM

No. 5

No. 5

No. 5

LAY ON FOLD

No. 3

78

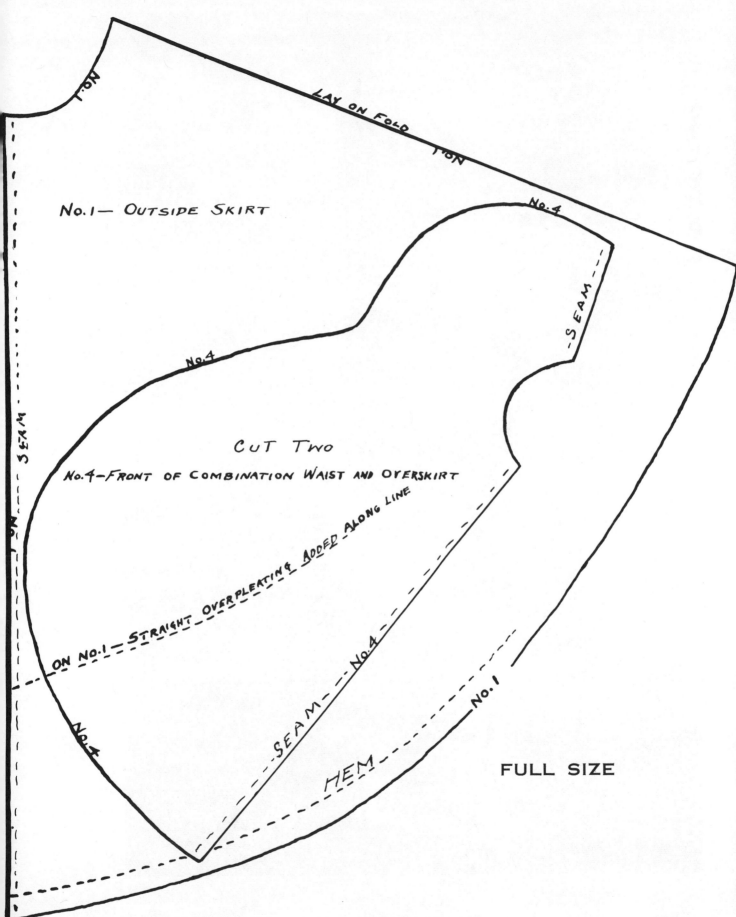

No. 1 — OUTSIDE SKIRT

No. 4

No. 4

CUT TWO

No. 4 — FRONT OF COMBINATION WAIST AND OVERSKIRT

ON NO. 1 — STRAIGHT OVERPLEATING ADDED ALONG LINE

No. 1

SEAM

No. 4

No. 1

SEAM — No. 4

HEM

No. 4

LAY ON FOLD

SEAM ON NO. 1

No. 4 — SEAM

FULL SIZE

79

BROWN LADY — Promenade 1870.

MATERIAL NEEDED:

Golden-brown taffeta silk; one-fourth inch wide orange-brown tinsel ribbon; bronze beads; three small pearl buttons; lace.

HOW TO MAKE:

Make the usual basic undergarments, according to the directions outlined on page 57, including the "C" type crinoline underskirt for stiffening as shown on Plate #3, page 66.

PATTERN PART #1: Cut dress skirt from the brown taffeta silk. Make seam at back and a ¼ inch hem at bottom. Fashion a ½ inch ruffle from a 4 inch wide piece of the same material into ¼ inch pleats to fit bottom of garment. Press, and sew in place around bottom of skirt, with heading. Next, make six small bows of orange-brown tinsel ribbon and tack them to front, back, and sides at heading. Fasten finished garment to doll.

PATTERN PARTS #2 AND #3: Cut out the waist from the brown taffeta silk. Close seams. Trim flowing sleeves with ruffles of brown silk. Fasten a piece of same material tightly around each arm from wrist to elbow, edging with a bit of white lace at the bottom. Fasten waist tightly to doll at waistline. Sew orange-brown ribbon to front and back of waist to resemble a yoke. Place a narrow band of ribbon around the neck. Arrange three small white pearl buttons down front of waist above yoke line. Make a strand of small bronze beads for a necklace.

PATTERN PARTS #4 AND #5: Cut out front and back panniers from the brown taffeta silk. Hem edges as shown and add ½ inch pleated ruffles around both, heading them with a trimming of ribbon sewed on flat. On each side of front pannier sew a small bow of orange-brown ribbon. Gather at tops and fasten in place at front and back.

PATTERN PART #6: Cut long back pannier from the same taffeta material. Sew ½ inch pleated ruffle on rounded side only of this pannier. Trim with ribbon at top of ruffle sewed on flat. Pleat at top and sew at each side of back so that pannier fans out from the center.

PATTERN PART #7: Cut out top back pannier from the same brown taffeta silk. Hem and add ½ inch pleated ruffle headed with ribbon sewed on flat. Gather at top; sew to waist and finish with a band of folded silk for a belt. Add small ribbon bow at center back.

HAT:

Cut out two round pieces of brown taffeta silk 2¼ inches in diameter. Slip-stitch together and press. Fold each side to top center and tack. Combine rosette or ribbon and feathers; sew on hat. Fasten on head at an angle.

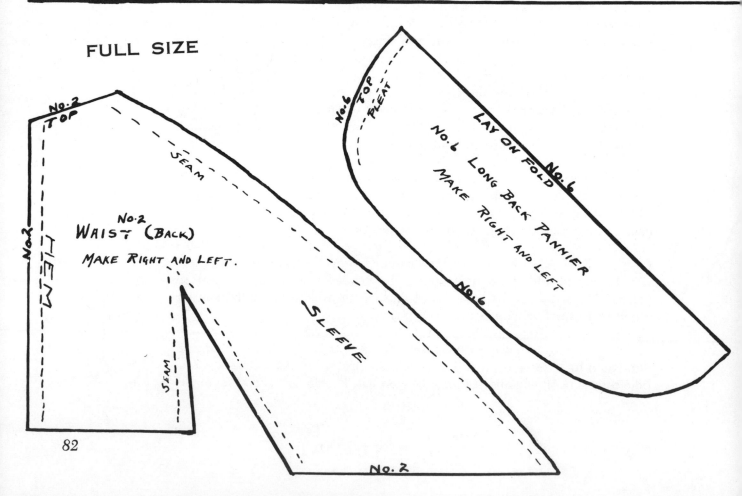

No.1 — TOP SKIRT

LAY ON FOLD No.1

HEM
No.1

FULL SIZE

No.2
TOP

SEAM

No.2
HEM

No.2
WAIST (BACK)
MAKE RIGHT AND LEFT.

SEAM

SLEEVE

No.2

No.6
TOP
PLEAT

LAY ON FOLD No.6

No.6 LONG BACK PANNIER
MAKE RIGHT AND LEFT

No.6

82

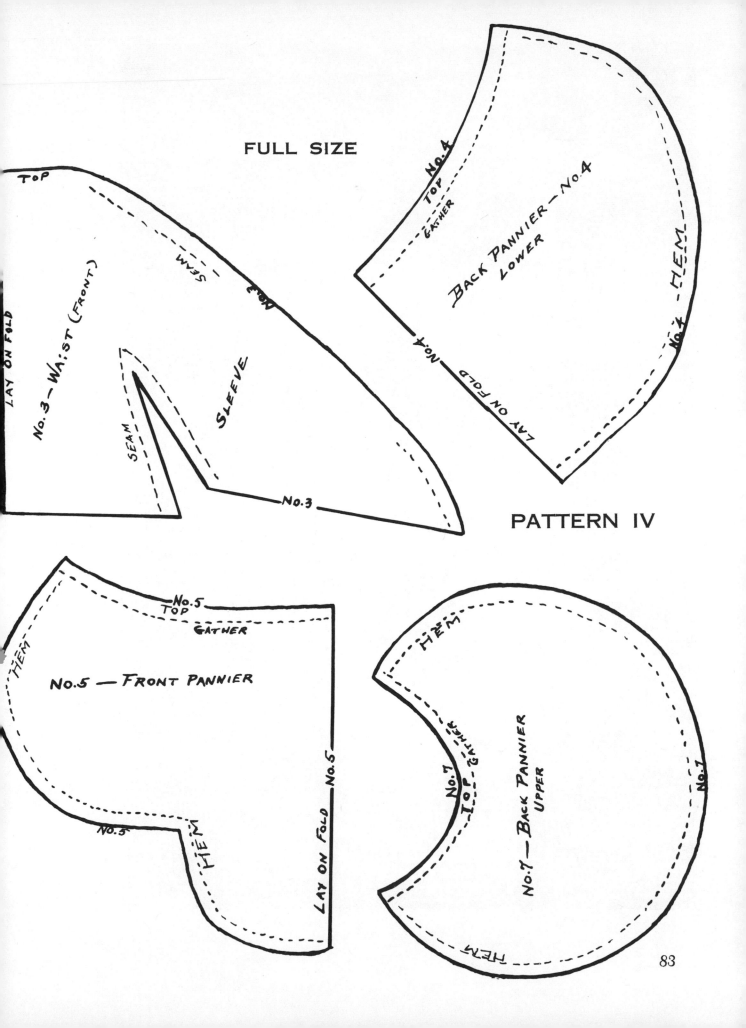

FULL SIZE

PATTERN IV

83

GODEY LADY DOLL DRESS PATTERN #5:

GOLDEN BROWN LADY — Walking Dress 1874.

MATERIAL NEEDED:

Golden colored silk; dark brown silk for trimming; dozen and a half small buttons covered with dark brown silk; brown beads.

HOW TO MAKE:

Make and fasten to doll according to directions on page 52, basic undergarments, including crinoline underskirt "B" as outlined on Plate #2, page 64.

PATTERN PART #1: Cut out dress skirt from the golden colored silk. Sew the dress skirt to the crinoline skirt. Make three double pleated ruffles from the dark brown silk — each to be 1¼ inches wide. Fasten them onto the golden silk skirt in rounded rows as indicated on pattern. For trimming, sew a ¼ inch bias strip of gold silk to the top of each ruffle. Fashion a number of ¼ inch bias strips of the dark brown silk, and sew them diagonally across front of gold silk skirt. Fasten skirt to doll.

PATTERN PART #2: Cut out two parts — a right and a left — of gold silk. Bind with dark brown silk on angle side only, placing a ¾ inch ruffle flat under binding. Sew on seven small brown silk covered buttons to each panel. Fasten to garment at each side of center front at slight angle. Close darts, gather and sew completed skirt to doll's body.

PATTERN PARTS #3, #4, #5 AND #6: Cut out jacket parts from the gold silk. Sew rounded part of gore #5 to back of jacket #3; seam sides and shoulders, leaving opening for sleeves. Make sleeves and sew into jacket. Face bottom of jacket with brown silk. Place simulated pockets at sides of jacket, with brown silk covered buttons for trim. Fit jacket to doll; close down front, sewing in place. Add two brown silk covered buttons below neck line for trim. Attach a ruffled neckpiece of gold and brown silk. Complete sleeves with double pleated ruffle divided by a narrow gold silk band for cuffs.

ACCESSORIES:

Make loops of small bronze beads for earrings and fasten in place. Make turban of brown silk and place double strand of bronze beads across front. Fasten to doll's hair.

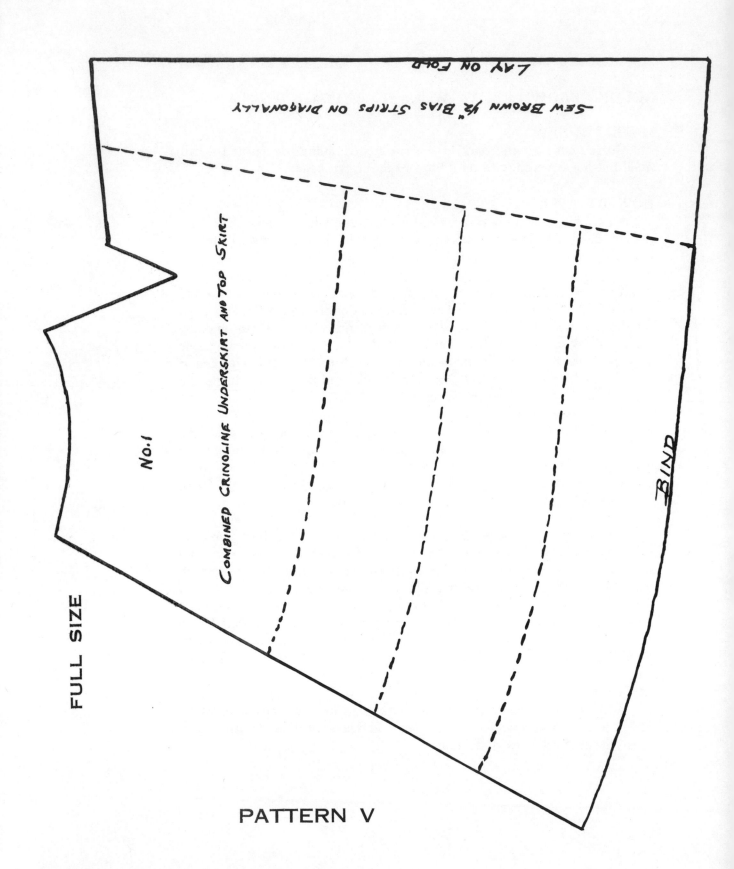

FULL SIZE

No. 1

COMBINED CRINOLINE UNDERSKIRT AND TOP SKIRT

SEW BROWN ½" BIAS STRIPS ON DIAGONALLY

LAY ON FOLD

BIND

PATTERN V

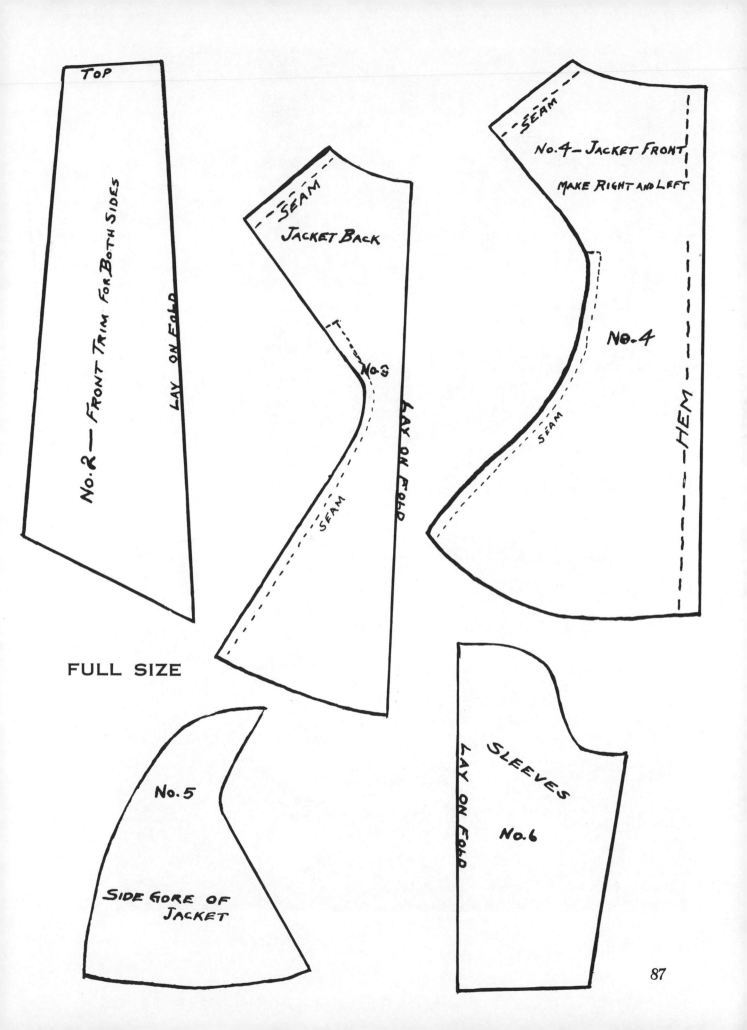

TOP

No. 2 — FRONT TRIM FOR BOTH SIDES

LAY ON FOLD

SEAM

JACKET BACK

No. 3

SEAM

LAY ON FOLD

FULL SIZE

SEAM

No. 4 — JACKET FRONT

MAKE RIGHT AND LEFT

No. 4

SEAM

HEM

No. 5

SIDE GORE OF JACKET

LAY ON FOLD

SLEEVES

No. 6

87

GODEY LADY DOLL DRESS PATTERN #6:

LAVENDER LADY — Ball Dress 1865.

MATERIAL NEEDED:

Pale lavender silk; cream silk lace 2½ inches wide with design; small silver or crystal beads.

HOW TO MAKE:

Make and sew onto doll, according to instructions on page 52, basic undergarments including crinoline underskirt, "B" found on Plate #2, page 64.

PATTERN PART #1: Cut out dress skirt from the pale lavender silk. Sew hem on bottom of skirt. Add a 1½ inch pleated ruffle cut from same material, and sew on bottom of dress. Then gather at waist and secure to doll.

PATTERN PARTS #2 AND #3: Cut out panniers from lavendar silk — a right and a left. Turn under front, bottom and back edges. Then, fold over corners of both panniers to position indicated on pattern part. Next, take a length of one inch lavender silk; fold over both edges; gather in center to make a ruching and sew all around on top of turned-under edges. After which, gather panniers at top and sew to waistline, having them meet in the back, fan shape, also furnishing a fan shaped effect in front.

PATTERN PART #4: Cut out sleeves from the cream silk lace material. Before seaming, make two ¼ inch tucks lengthwise of sleeves. Then, take a length of folded-over lavender silk trim and insert plain between each tuck with French knots of pale lavender thread. Finish by seaming sleeves and fastening them securely to shoulders.

PATTERN PARTS #5 AND #6: Cut out waist from the cream silk lace material. Seam shoulders. Next, tuck back and front parts of waist as indicated; fit and tack to doll at neck, shoulders, and under arms to meet dress sleeves. Gather at waistline. Next, make a ¼ inch wide band of lavender material — cut on bias — and fasten with French knots of pale lavender thread over shoulders to simulate yoke, back and front. Make a belt of folded lavender silk and fasten around waist with French knots. Add a small flat bow of same material at center back. Trim around neck with gathered lace. Secure a band of black silk cord high up around the neck from which suspends a strand of crystal or silver beads for a pendant.
HEADDRESS:

Use a circle of silver or crystal beads entwined with tiny flowers.

FULL SIZE

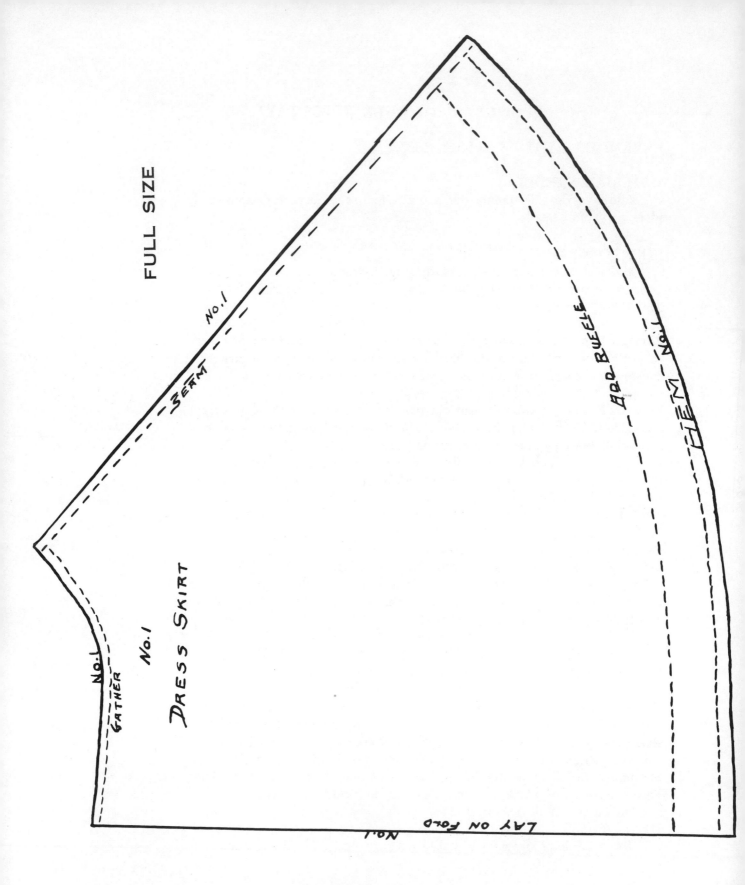

No.1

SEAM

GATHER No.1

No.1

DRESS SKIRT

ADD RUFFLE

HEM

LAY ON FOLD No.1

PATTERN VI

90

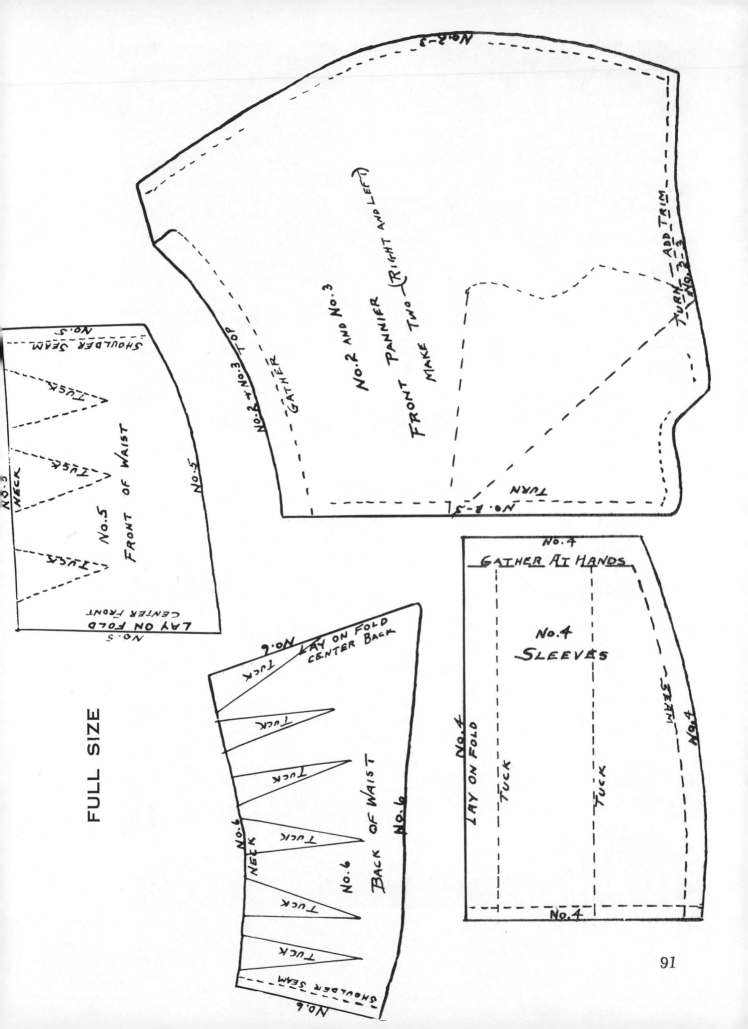

FULL SIZE

No.2-3

No.2 AND No.3
FRONT PANNIER (RIGHT AND LEFT)
MAKE TWO

TURN — ADD TRIM
No. 2-3

No.2+No.3 TOP
GATHER

TURN
No.2-3

SHOULDER SEAM
No.5

TUCK
TUCK
TUCK

NECK
No.5

No.5
FRONT OF WAIST

No.5
LAY ON FOLD
CENTER FRONT

No.6
LAY ON FOLD
CENTER BACK
TUCK
TUCK
TUCK
TUCK

No.6
NECK

No.6
BACK OF WAIST
No.6

TUCK
TUCK

SHOULDER SEAM
No.6

No.4
GATHER AT HANDS

No.4
SLEEVES

LAY ON FOLD
No.4
TUCK
TUCK

SEAM
No.4

No.4

91

ROSE LACE LADY — Afternoon Dress, 1874.

MATERIAL NEEDED:
  Rose taffeta silk; ecru lace; crystal brooch.

HOW TO MAKE:
  Make and sew onto doll according to instructions on page 52, basic undergarments, including crinoline underskirt "B" as shown on Plate #2, page 64.

PATTERN PART #1: Cut out the outside skirt from rose taffeta silk. Face bottom with one inch strip of same material cut on bias. Gather at waistline and sew to doll.

PATTERN PART #2: Cut out back pannier from rose taffeta. Hem bottom. Edge bottom with two pieces of ecru lace stitched together at selvage and gathered. Make upward pleats, as indicated on pattern part. Gather at waistline and sew to doll. Gather ½ inch wide ecru lace on each side of ¼ inch ecru lace insertion four inches long, forming a rounded corner at bottom. Sew down center back of pannier for trimming. (Front and back panniers are attached, at sides.)

PATTERN PART #3: Cut out on the bias, from taffeta silk, the front pannier. Edge bottom with two pieces of ¼ inch wide ecru lace sewed along selvage edges and gathered. Make upward pleats, as indicated. Gather pannier at waistline and tack to doll. Next, gather one-half inch ecru lace on each side of ¼ inch insertion, four inches long, forming a rounded corner at bottom. Sew down front center. Now, make two more pieces of similar trimming three inches long and sew them down each side where front and back panniers join.

PATTERN PART #4: Cut waist out of the taffeta silk. Close seams. Make a ¼ inch strip of silk edged with gathered lace and sew down center of sleeves with French knots. Slip over doll's head, and gather at neck and waist. Make revers to go over each shoulder front and back with ruffled lace tacked to each side of ¼ inch insertions. Next, prepare a strip of ¼ inch wide silk folded. Stitch down center front of waist with French knots of rose colored thread. Band neck with ecru lace insertion.
HEADDRESS:
  Sew together two pieces of ¼ inch ecru lace, five inches long; tack beads and French knots on alternately; festoon over head from front to back. Use a small crystal ornament for brooch.

93

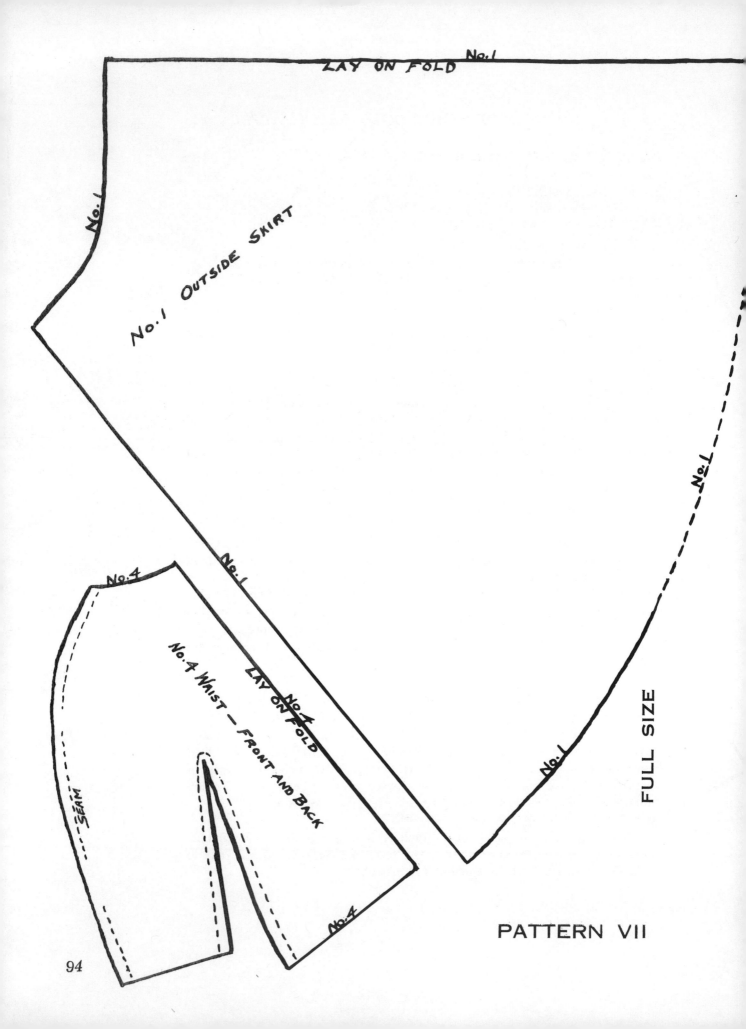

LAY ON FOLD No.1

No.1

No.1 OUTSIDE SKIRT

No.1

No.1

No.4

No.4 WAIST — FRONT AND BACK

LAY ON FOLD

No.4

SEAM

No.4

No.1

FULL SIZE

PATTERN VII

94

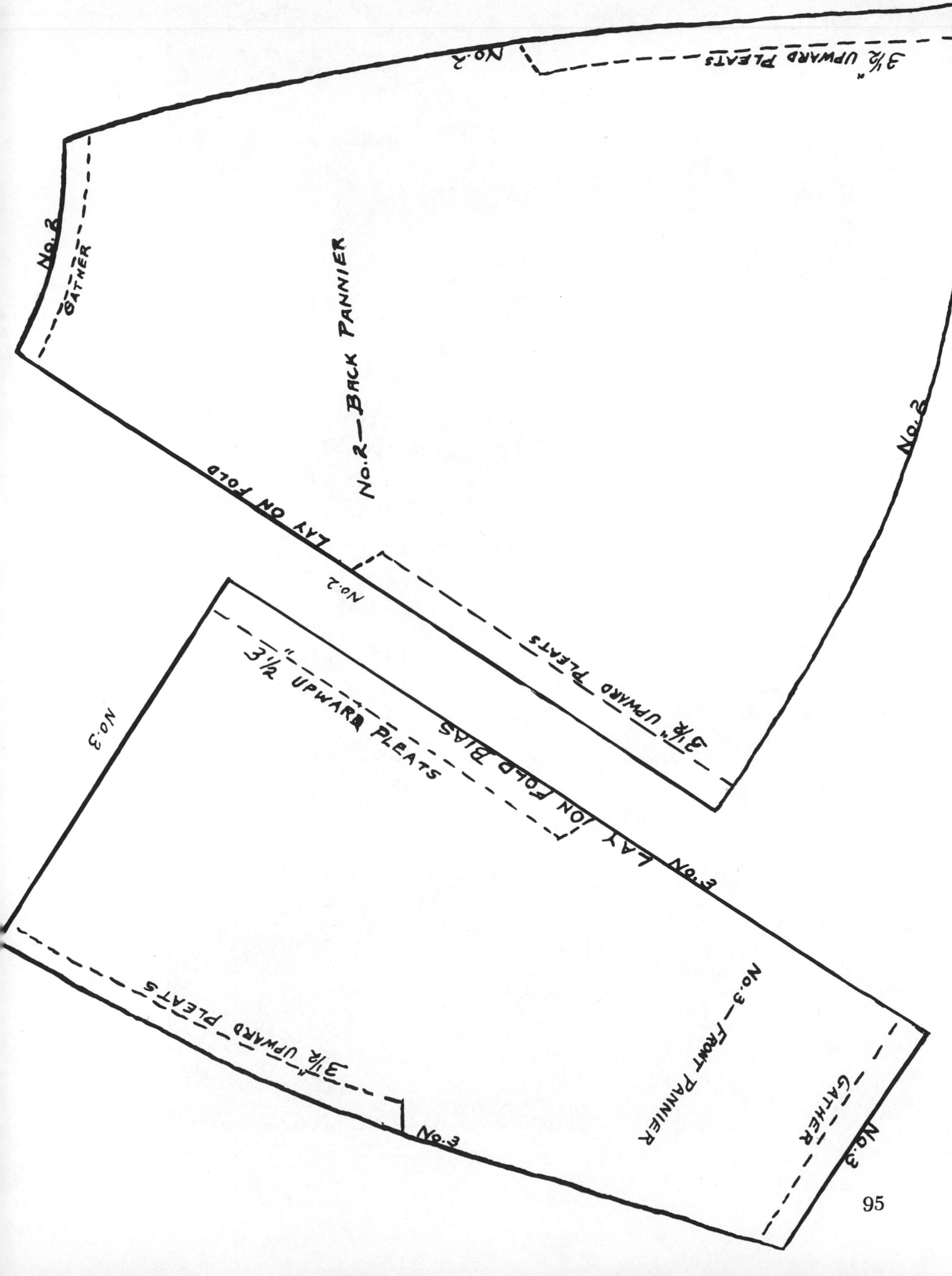

No.2

3½" UPWARD PLEATS

No.2

GATHER

No.2 — BACK PANNIER

LAY ON FOLD

No.2

No.2

3½" UPWARD PLEATS

3½" UPWARD PLEATS

No.3

3½" UPWARD PLEATS

LAY ON FOLD BIAS

No.3

No.3 — FRONT PANNIER

3½" UPWARD PLEATS

No.3

GATHER

No.3

95

GODEY LADY DOLL DRESS PATTERN #8:

BLACK AND PLAID LADY — Watering Place Dress 1864.

MATERIAL NEEDED:

Black-and-white checked silk; black plush; jet beads; small gold beads; black soutache braid.

HOW TO MAKE:

Make and fit to doll, according to instructions on page 52, basic undergarments including crinoline underskirt "C" as shown on Plate 3, page 66.

PATTERN PART #1: Cut out dress skirt from the black-and-white checked silk. Hem and pleat as shown and sew to crinoline underskirt at bottom. After completion, secure to doll.

PATTERN PART #2: Cut out the upper part of outside skirt from the black-and-white checked material on the bias. Gather at top and bottom and sew to crinoline skirt, over part 1.

PATTERN PARTS #3, #4 AND #5: Cut out the jacket from black plush. Seam sides and shoulders; make darts; and face bottom with black satin. Make and sew sleeves in place. One-half inch from the bottom, trim jacket with round or square design as desired, using black soutache braid. Bind neck with ¼ inch wide strip of same material. Sew jacket down the front. Use gold bead necklace for neck trim.

MUFF:

Make a roll of heavy black satin edged with band of plush at each end. Fill center with cotton; secure doll's left hand in muff; and sew to waistline center.

HAT:

From a heavy writing paper, cut out a circle three inches in diameter. Cover top part with black plush — on underside use cerise-colored satin. Circle hat from top to bottom with ½ inch cerise satin ribbon and tie with bow under chin at the side. Add small ostrich feathers — black and cerise — at left side on top.

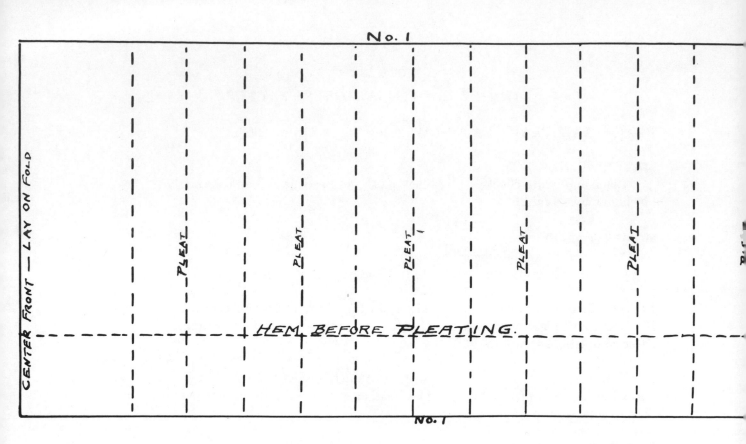

No. 1

CENTER FRONT — LAY ON FOLD

PLEAT

PLEAT

PLEAT

PLEAT

PLEAT

HEM BEFORE PLEATING.

No. 1

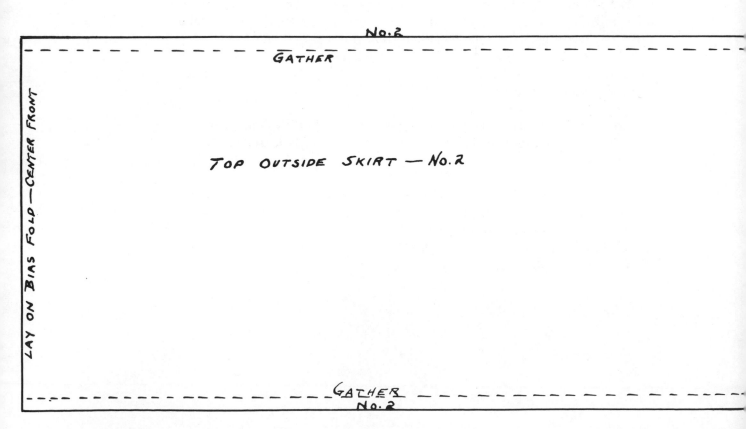

No. 2

GATHER

LAY ON BIAS FOLD — CENTER FRONT

TOP OUTSIDE SKIRT — No. 2

GATHER
No. 2

PATTERN VIII

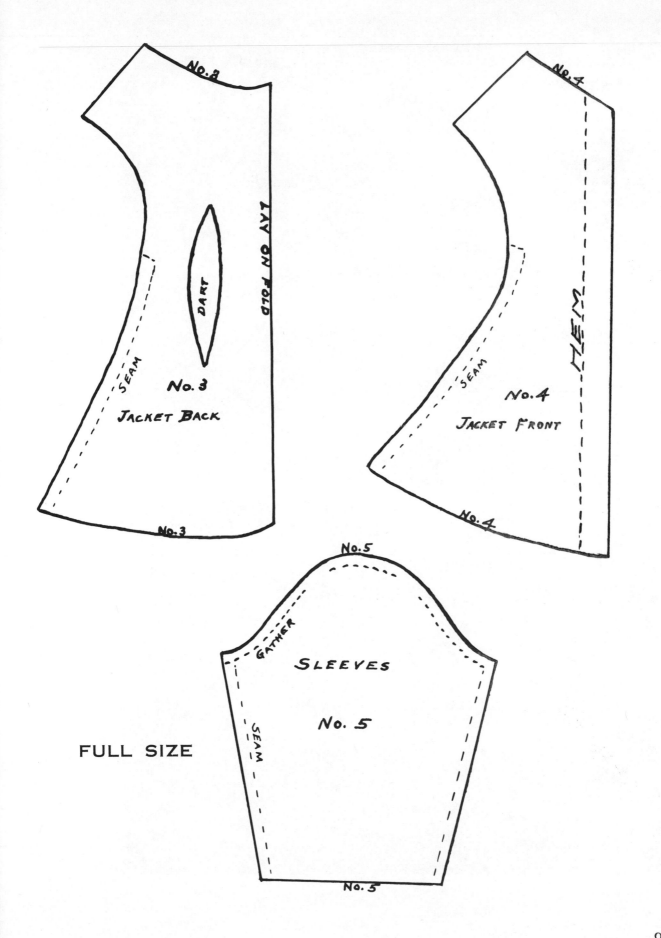

FULL SIZE

99

GODEY LADY DOLL DRESS PATTERN #9:

BLACK AND FUCHSIA LADY — Walking Dress, 1871.

MATERIAL NEEDED:
Fuchsia-colored silk; black-and-grey striped silk $\frac{1}{16}$ inch wide; old-gold colored beads; white satin; black silk lace ½ inch and 1½ inches wide.

HOW TO MAKE:
Make and fit to doll, according to directions on page 52, basic undergarments, including crinoline underskirt for stiffening designated by "B" on Plate 2, page 64.

PATTERN PART #1: Cut out dress skirt from the fuchsia-colored silk. Close seam and hem. Using same material 3 inches wide, hem and pleat, and add to bottom. Gather and secure at waistline.

PATTERN PART #2: Cut out the dickie from white satin, making a right and a left. Hem front edges and sew on top of hem a flat strip of ¼ inch black lace. Face neckline with white satin. Fasten to doll.

PATTERN PARTS #3, #4 AND #5: Cut out cape from the black and grey silk. Seam sides and shoulders; make darts and hem bottoms; face corners with white satin; sew gathered black lace around corners; fold over at dotted line and tack to dickie. Edge bottom of cape with the 1½ inch wide black lace pleated at intervals to fit bottom — lace to be long at back and short in front. Next, seam sleeves; fashion cuffs from crosswise pieces of striped silk. Around bottom, sew ¼ inch wide black lace gathered. Finish neckline with ¼ inch wide pleated white satin. Draw cape together at center front and tack. Make strand of old-gold beads for necklace.

HEADDRESS:
Prepare a rosette of black lace and attach to hair at forehead; from rosette, drape streamers of black lace down back of head.

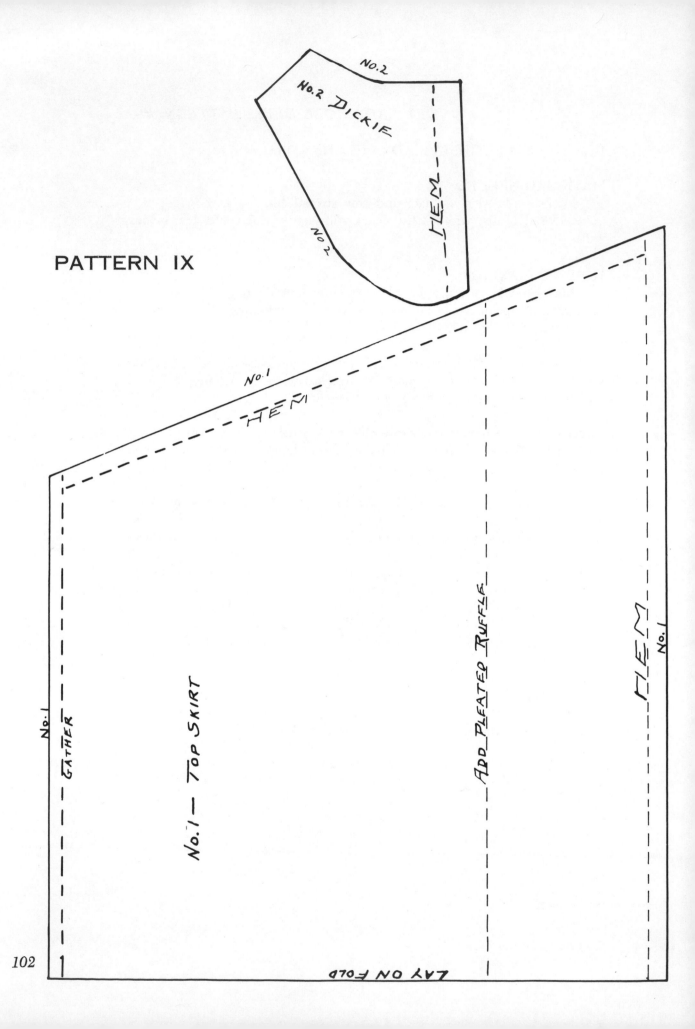

PATTERN IX

No.2 DICKIE

No. 2

No. 2

HEM

No. 1

HEM

No. 1

GATHER

No. 1 — TOP SKIRT

ADD PLEATED RUFFLE

HEM

No. 1

LAY ON FOLD

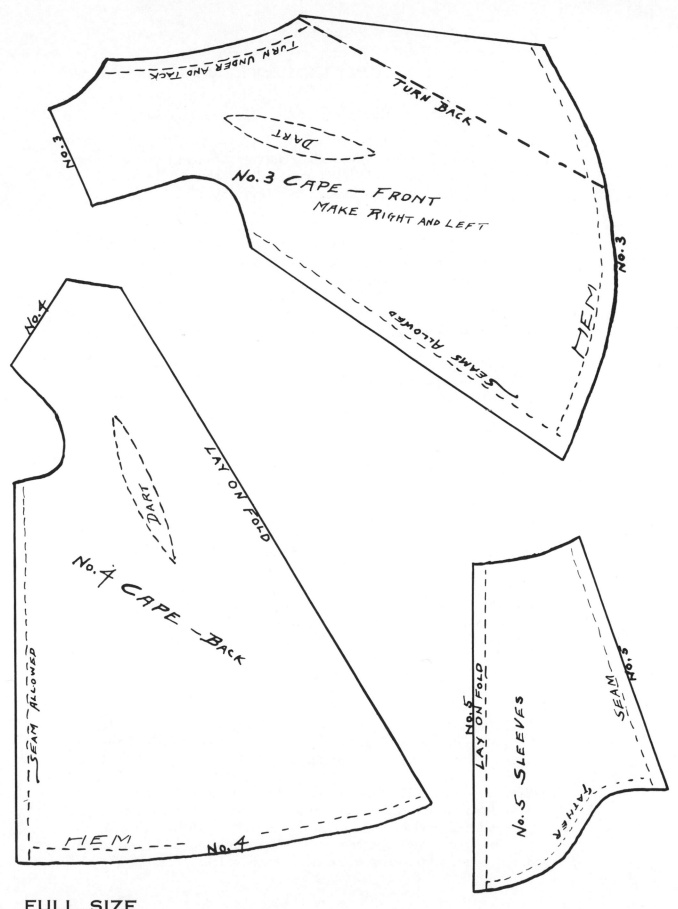

No. 3 CAPE — FRONT
MAKE RIGHT AND LEFT

TURN UNDER AND TACK

TURN BACK

DART

No. 3

HEM   No. 3

SEAMS ALLOWED

No. 4

No. 4 CAPE — BACK

DART

LAY ON FOLD

SEAM ALLOWED

HEM   No. 4

No. 5 SLEEVES

No. 5

LAY ON FOLD

SEAM   No. 5

GATHER

FULL SIZE

103

YOUNG GIRL — Mayday dress 1865.

MATERIAL NEEDED:

Fine striped robin-egg blue silk; light grey satin; white tucked dimity; white lace; small round black silk cord; red-and-white striped material for hose; black kid leather for boots; black satin ribbon.

HOW TO MAKE:

Make pantalettes and organdy underskirt two inches shorter than dimensions shown on basic patterns, page 57. Follow closely instructions covering pattern parts #1 to #16.

PATTERN PART #1: Cut out bustle from white organdy, and pad with cotton. Tack to doll.

PATTERN PART #2: Cut out crinoline underskirt; seam and close darts; fold over material on offset marked "A", and tack: bind bottom with blue silk. Attach skirt to doll.

PATTERN PART #3: Cut out dress skirt from the blue striped silk material. Seam and hem; fasten garment to doll, allowing lace border of organdy underskirt to show below hem.

PATTERN PARTS #4, #5 AND #6: Cut out crinoline base for pannier puffs, as per part #4; next, cut out, from the grey silk, panniers, as per parts #5 and #6; draw together to make puffs; fasten #5 to crinoline foundation, and sew #6 on the top of #5; then, fasten to waistline in back. Finish up by placing a small bit of cotton under each puff.

PATTERN PARTS #7, #8 AND #9: Cut out crinoline foundation, as per part #7, for side pannier puffs; close dart; then, cut panniers, from the grey silk material, as per pattern parts #8 and #9; draw together to make puffs; next, attach puff #8 to crinoline foundation, and sew #9 on top of #8; fasten at sides to waistline. Finish by placing bits of cotton under each puff.

PATTERN PART #10: Cut out apron from the grey silk. Make double. Following design shown on pattern part #10, sew on black-cord trimming; tack to waistline and side panniers.

PATTERN PARTS #11, #12 AND #13: Inner waist and sleeves. Cut out waist from tucked white dimity. Seam shoulders and under arms of parts #11 and #12; make sleeves and gather at wrists with ¼ inch white lace; sew onto waist. Next, gather material at neckline, and add band of white dimity edged with narrow white lace. Attach to doll.

104

PATTERN PARTS #14, #15 AND #16: Outer waist and sleeves. Cut these out of the grey silk. Seam shoulders and under arms; make and sew in sleeves. Trim waist, as shown on pattern part #14, with black cord; gather sleeves at bottom; add band of grey silk ½ inch wide and border with double row of black cord about ⅛ inch apart. Make two shoulder straps with trimming, as shown in design, pattern part #16, extending over shoulders from front to back waistline.

STOCKINGS:

Make out of red-and-white striped material and fit to leg.

BOOTS:

As per pattern part #6 shown on Plate #1, page ——, cut out boots from black kid leather (an old kid glove will do); fit to feet and whipstitch together.

HEADDRESS:

Make a bow of ½ inch wide black satin ribbon; attach to hair, with loops standing up fanwise, and streamers extending down back of head.   *105*

PATTERN X

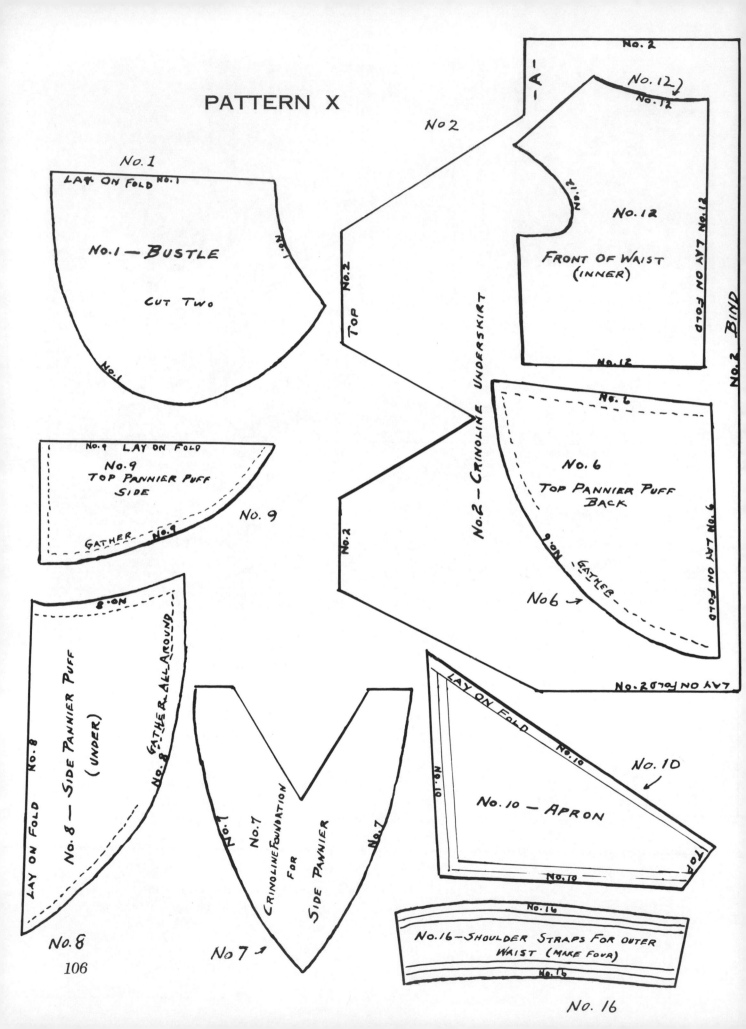

No. 1 — BUSTLE
CUT TWO
LAY ON FOLD No. 1

No. 2 — Crinoline Underskirt
Top No. 2
BIND No. 2

No. 12
FRONT OF WAIST (INNER)
LAY ON FOLD No. 12

No. 9 LAY ON FOLD
No. 9 TOP PANNIER PUFF SIDE
GATHER No. 9

No. 6 TOP PANNIER PUFF BACK
LAY ON FOLD No. 6
GATHER No. 6

No. 8 — SIDE PANNIER PUFF (UNDER)
LAY ON FOLD No. 8
GATHER ALL AROUND

No. 7 CRINOLINE FOUNDATION FOR SIDE PANNIER

No. 10 — APRON
LAY ON FOLD No. 10

No. 16 — SHOULDER STRAPS FOR OUTER WAIST (MAKE FOUR)

106

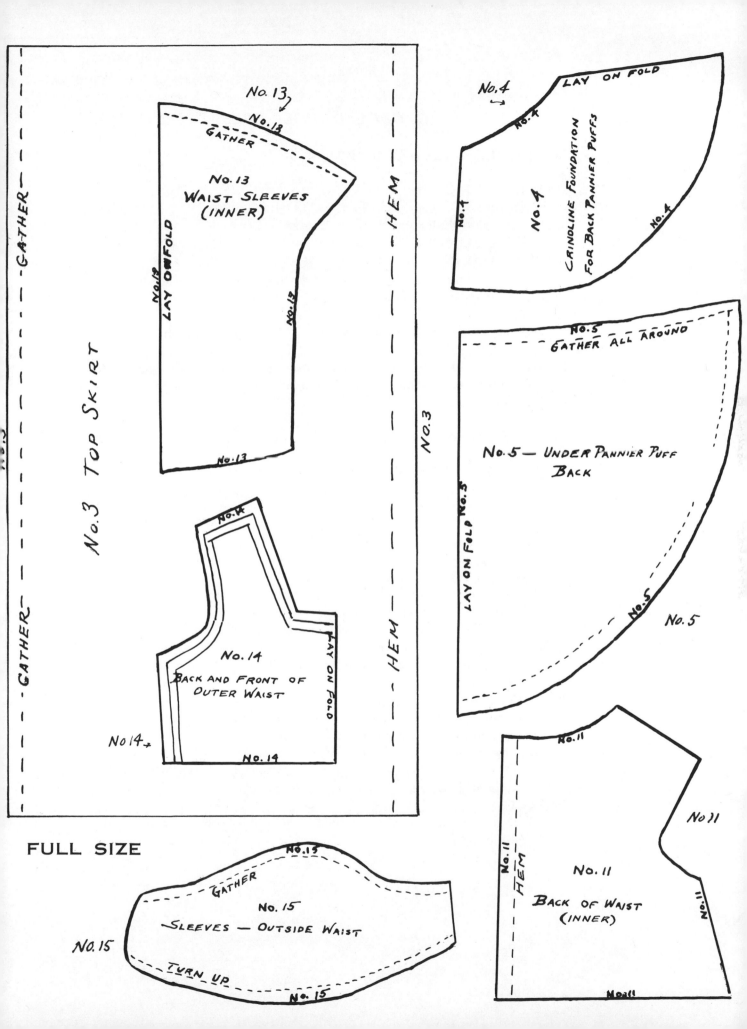

No. 13

No. 13

GATHER

No. 13
WAIST SLEEVES
(INNER)

LAY ON FOLD
No. 13

No. 13

No. 13

No. 4
LAY ON FOLD

No. 4

No. 4

No. 4

CRINOLINE FOUNDATION
FOR BACK PANNIER PUFFS

No. 4

GATHER

No. 3 TOP SKIRT

HEM

No. 3

No. 3

No. 5
GATHER ALL AROUND

No. 5 — UNDER PANNIER PUFF
BACK

LAY ON FOLD No. 5

No. 5

No. 5

No. 14

No. 14
BACK AND FRONT OF
OUTER WAIST

LAY ON FOLD

No. 14

No. 14

No. 14

No. 11

No. 11

No. 11
BACK OF WAIST
(INNER)

No. 11
HEM

No. 11

No. 11

FULL SIZE

No. 15

GATHER

No. 15
SLEEVES — OUTSIDE WAIST

No. 15

TURN UP

No. 15

ROSE GOLD LADY — Walking Dress, 1870.

MATERIAL NEEDED:

Soft, rose silk; gold lace, four inches wide, of delicate design and mesh; extra fine flesh-colored silk net; gold beads.

HOW TO MAKE:

Cut out, make and sew to doll, according to directions on page 52, basic undergarments, including crinoline underskirt "A" as show on Plate one, page 62.

Follow closely instructions covering pattern parts one to three.

PATTERN PART #1: Cut out top skirt from the soft rose silk; make hem around bottom two inches wide; pleat in circle about waistline, and attach to doll.

PATTERN PARTS #2 AND #3: Before cutting out waist, prepare doll's shoulders, neck, and arms as follows:

Sew a piece of the gold net to doll's neck and shoulders, simulating a yoke; using same material, stitch to arms a piece extending from elbows to wrists, forming puff effect; next, fasten a narrow band of rose silk around neck and at bottom of sleeves. Now, cut out drop-shoulder waist from the rose silk material. Seam shoulders and under arms; gather and turn under at neck; attach to doll. Fasten bottom of sleeves at elbows over the gold silk net puffs.

Drape a piece of the gold lace, four inches wide by nine inches long, around shoulders; tack ends at waistline. Next, fashion two streamers of same material — one, 1¼ inches wide by 2½ inches long, the other, the same width by 3½ inches long; whip edges and allow to extend down front of dress; make a small rosette of rose silk and tack it in center front at junction of shoulder drape and streamers.

HEADDRESS:

Cut out a circle of fine black felt four and one-fourth inches in diameter; dampen felt and shape to head; when dry, trim with a festoon of tiny flowers across the top; tack two small flowers — one right and the other left — on front, under side of hat. Fit and fasten on with narrow black velvet ribbon ties.

BASKET:

Shop around and purchase a small basket: fill with tiny flowers, and hang on doll's arm.

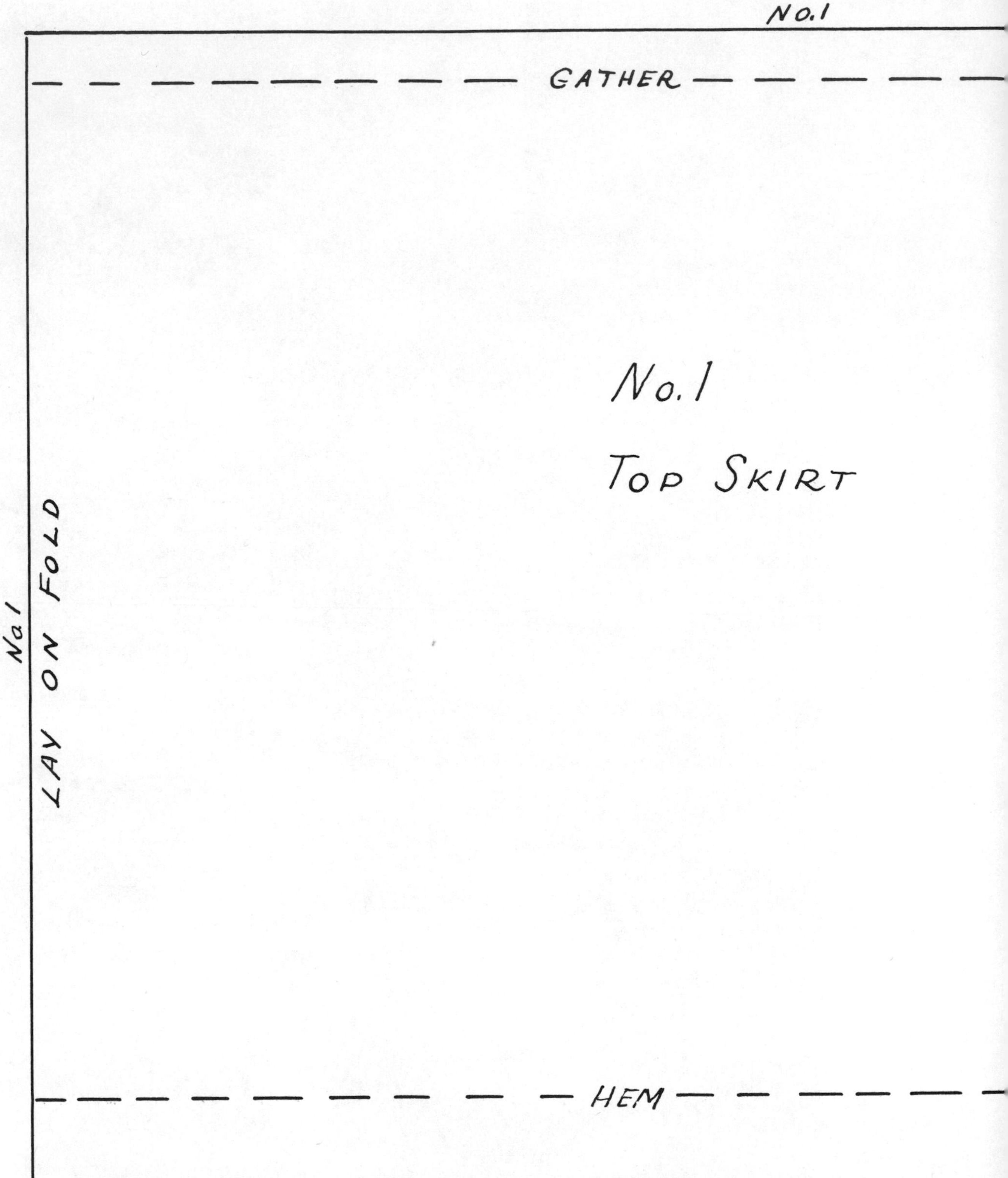
No.1
GATHER
No.1
TOP SKIRT
No.1
LAY ON FOLD
HEM
No.1

FULL SIZE

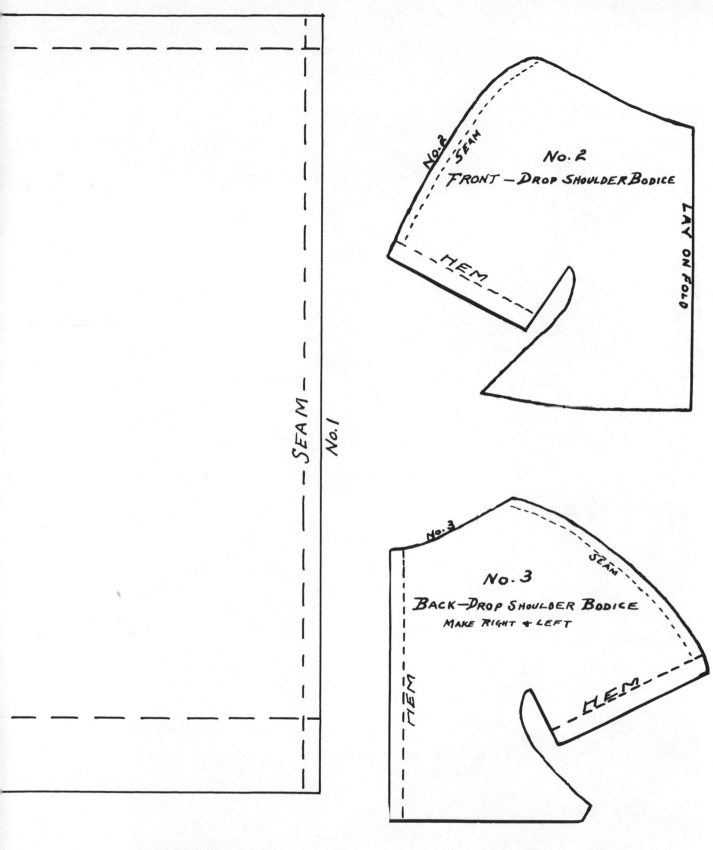

SEAM
No. 1

No. 2
No. 2
SEAM
FRONT — DROP SHOULDER BODICE
HEM
LAY ON FOLD

No. 3
No. 3
SEAM
No. 3
BACK — DROP SHOULDER BODICE
MAKE RIGHT & LEFT
HEM
HEM

PATTERN XI

111

GODEY LADY DOLL DRESS PATTERN #12:

NILE GREEN LADY — Promenade dress, 1865.

MATERIAL NEEDED:

Light green satin; black silk lace with flower design; black silk lace 1½ inches wide; black veiling; white seed pearls.

HOW TO MAKE:

Cut out and fit to doll, according to directions on Plate 1, page 62, basic undergarments, including crinoline underskirt "A" as described on page 52.

Follow descriptions covering pattern parts from #1 to #8.

PATTERN PART #1: Cut out the dress skirt from the nile green satin. Seam back and make 1½ inch hem at the bottom; gather at top and attach to doll.

PATTERN PARTS #2 AND #3: Cut out the back panniers from nile green satin. Gather sides and bottom; draw up to make puffs. Gather at top; fasten to doll, having panniers meet at front and back, spreading out fan-wise with puff effect around sides.

PATTERN PARTS #4 AND #5: Before cutting out waist, prepare doll's shoulders, neck, and arms as follows:

Sew a piece of cream net to doll's neck and shoulders, simulating a yoke; using same material, stitch to arms a piece extending from elbows to wrists, forming puff effect; next, fasten a narow band of nile green satin around neck and at bottom of sleeves. Now, cut out drop-shoulder waist from the nile green silk material. Seam shoulders and under arms; gather at elbows, also gather and turn under at neck, attach to doll. Fasten bottom of sleeves at elbows over the cream silk net puffs. Draw center front of waist down to a point over bust and tack a brooch of seed pearls in place.

PATTERN PART #6: Cut out mantilla from the flower-design black silk lace; edge all around with gathered black silk lace 1½ inches wide; lay in folds across shoulders, draping gracefully over arms between elbows and hands; fasten hands in place to hold mantilla in position.

PATTERN PARTS #7 AND #8: Cut out poke bonnet from the nile green satin. Use a piece of crinoline the size of bonnet brim, as shown by pattern part #8; slip-stitch on a covering of nile green satin; face bottom of bonnet curtain as directed on pattern part #7; gather at top and sew to back of brim; now, draw center of curtain tightly, and tack balance to each side of brim; attach to the doll. Arrange black veiling across face; tie on top of poke bonnet with splashy bow.

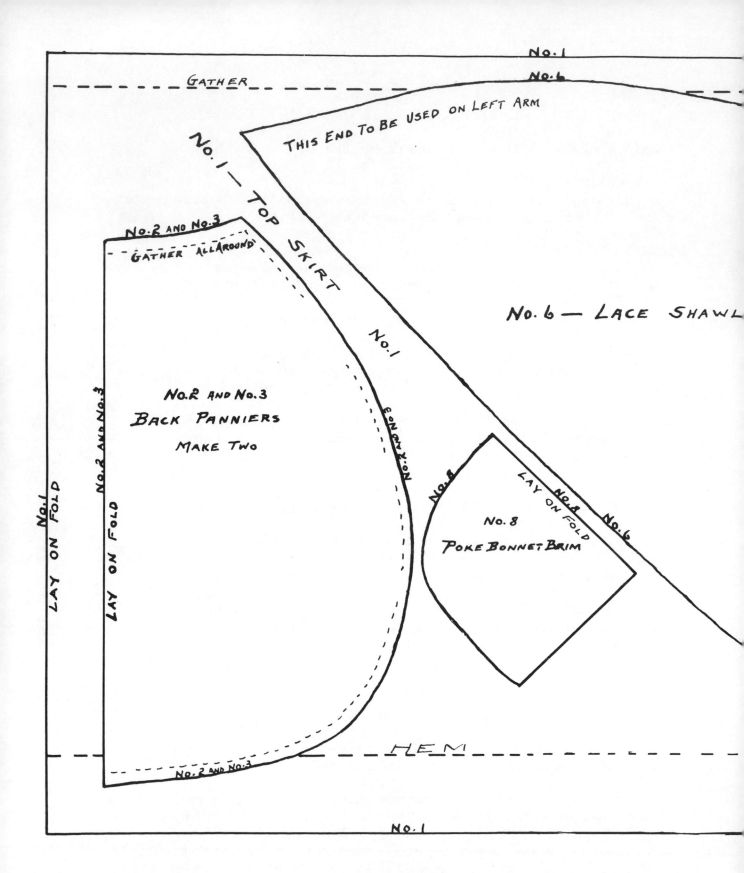

PATTERN XII

114

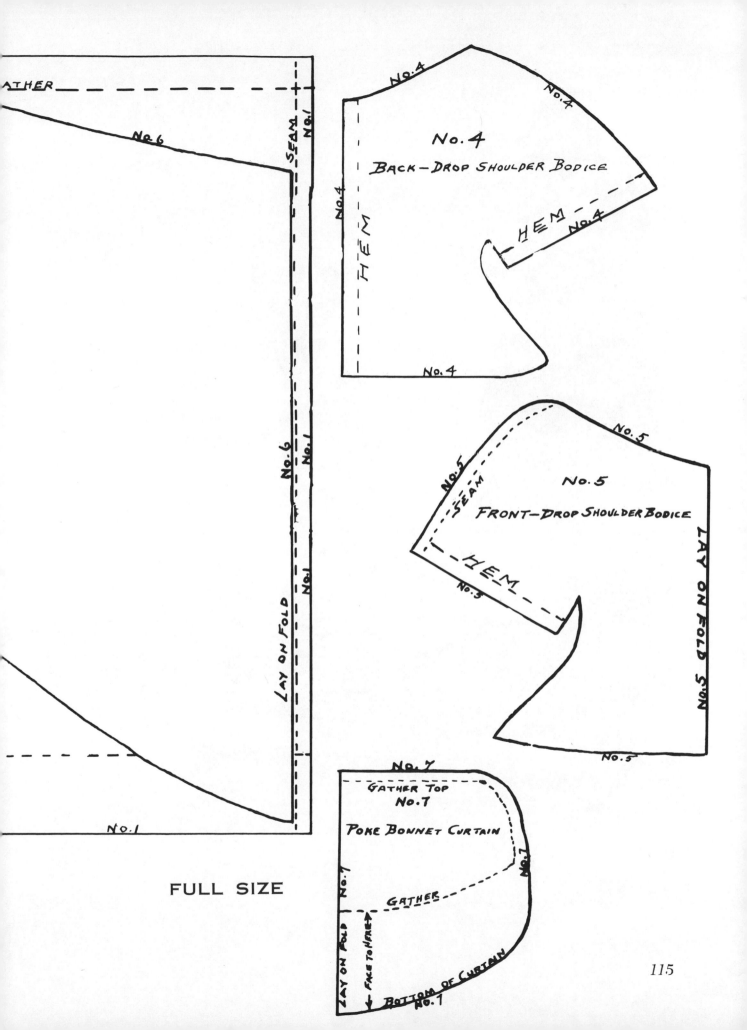

FULL SIZE

115

MAMMY — Maid costume, 1864.

MATERIAL NEEDED:
Red calico with small yellow and black design; white dimity; white lace 1¼ inches wide.

HOW TO MAKE:
Cut out, make and attach to doll the basic undergarments, as described and shown on Plates 1 and 3, pages 62 and 66, including crinoline underskirt "A", found on Plate 1. Follow carefully descriptions covering pattern parts #1 to #6.

PATTERN PART #1: Cut out the outside skirt from the red calico, according to note describing pattern part #1.

PATTERN PARTS #2 AND #3: Cut out waist from the red calico. Seam and close darts; hem fronts; gather at neckline and add narrow neck band. Draw together at waistline and sew to doll.

PATTERN PART #4: Cut out shoulder straps from white dimity; hem, fold into four pleats, and press; arrange over shoulders crosswise, and tack to dress back and front.

PATTERN PART #5: Cut out apron from white dimity. Hem sides and bottom, and sew on a plain border of white lace 1¼ inches wide; gather top edge into a belt; make two ties of white dimity 2½ inches wide by 6½ inches long; hem and attach to belt; tie around waist and fasten to doll.

PATTERN PART #6: Cut out the three-cornered cap, from calico. Make sure it is cut on the bias; sew a ¼ inch hem entirely around; tie the three corners together at front center, and attach to doll.

No. 1

NOTE:
PATTERN PART No. 1 — DRESS SKIRT —
CUT ON FOLD A RECTANGULAR STRIP OF CALICO
7½" WIDE BY 13" LONG. HEM BOTTOM AND
GATHER AT THE TOP.

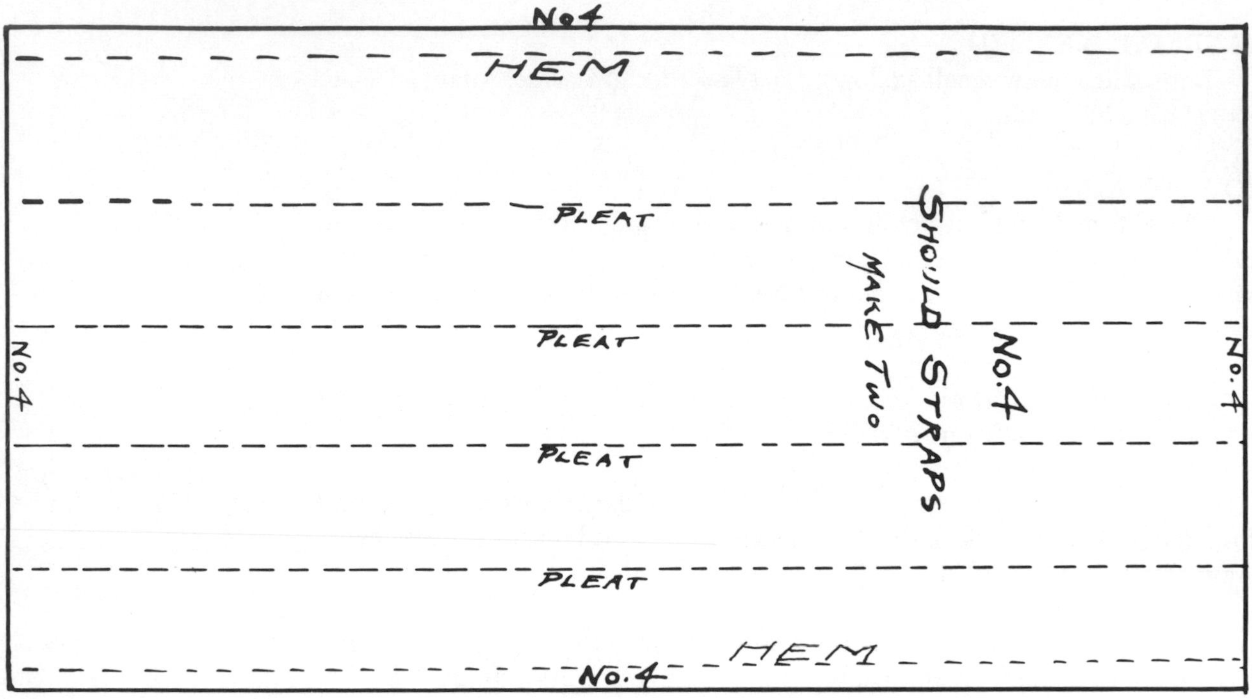

No. 4

HEM

PLEAT

PLEAT

No. 4

SHOULD STRAPS

MAKE TWO

No. 4

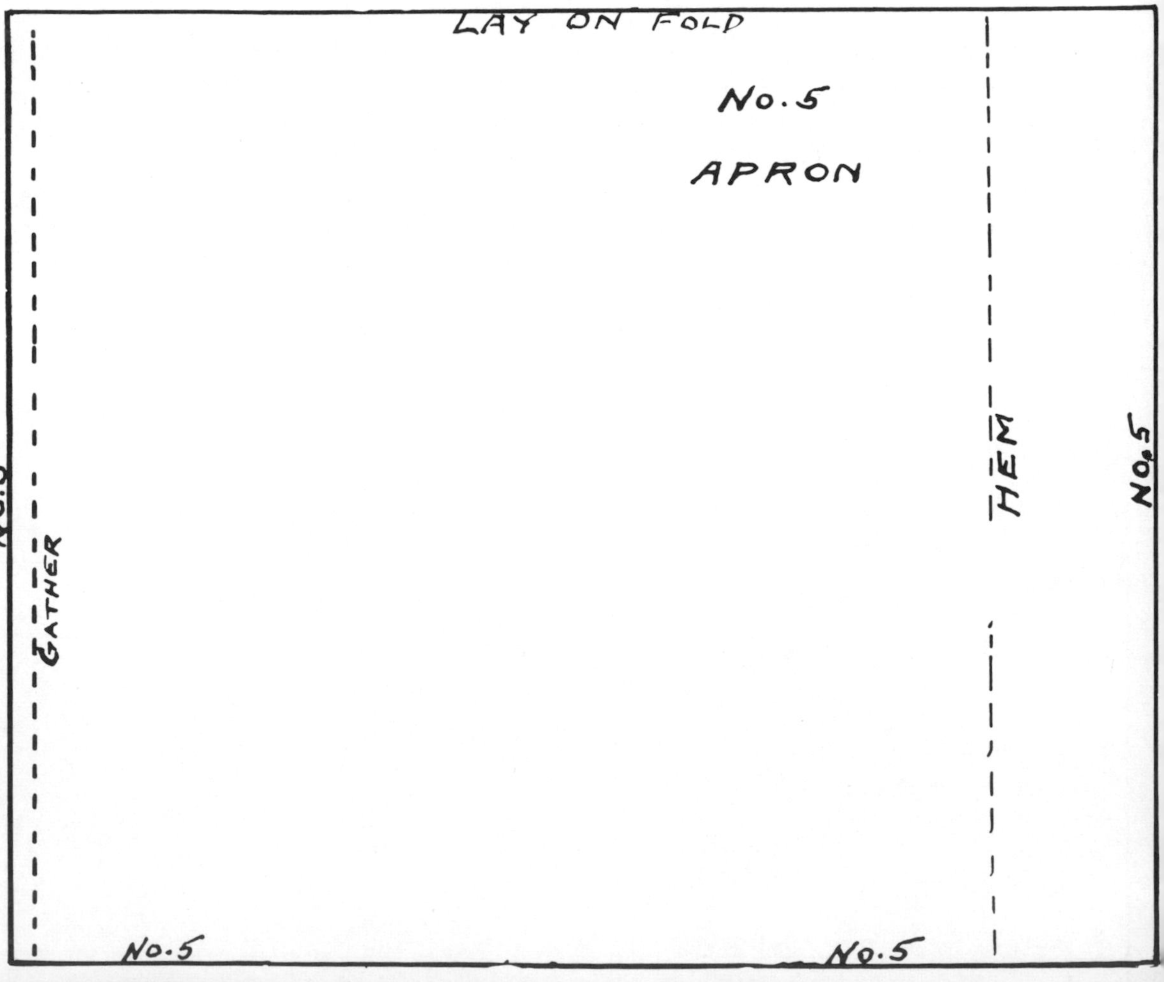

No. 4

PLEAT

PLEAT

HEM

No. 4

LAY ON FOLD

No. 5

APRON

No. 5

GATHER

HEM

No. 5

118

No. 5

No. 5

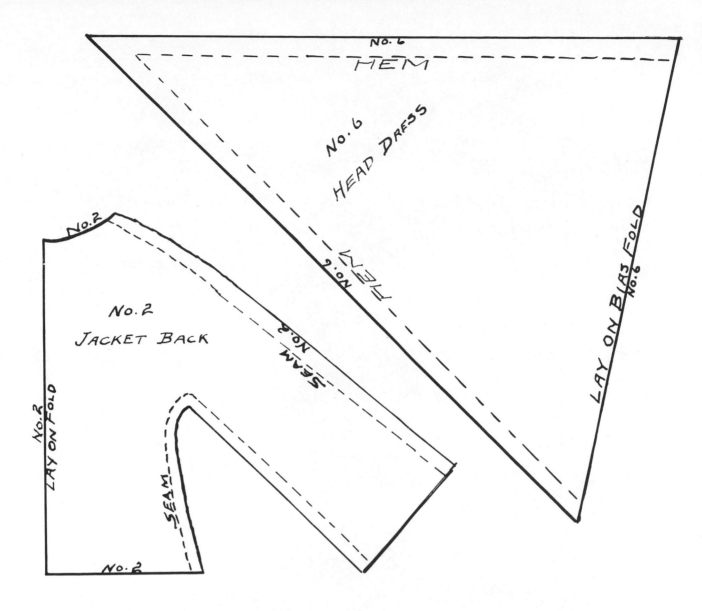

NO. 6
HEM

No. 6
HEAD DRESS

No. 2

SEAM No. 6

LAY ON BIAS FOLD
No. 6

No. 2
JACKET BACK

No. 2
LAY ON FOLD

SEAM

No. 2

FULL SIZE

PATTERN XIII

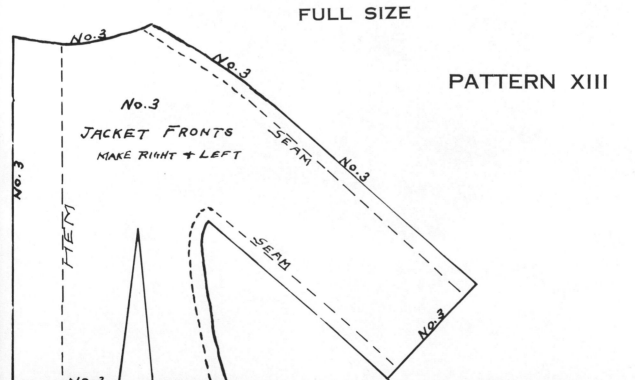

No. 3

No. 3

No. 3
JACKET FRONTS
MAKE RIGHT + LEFT

SEAM
No. 3

No. 3
HEM

SEAM

No. 3

No. 3

119

BLACK AND WHITE STRIPED LADY — Walking Dress, 1862.

MATERIAL NEEDED:

Black satin; black-and-white striped silk; heavy black plush; feather; bit of black lace.

HOW TO MAKE:

Cut out, make and attach to doll, following instructions as outlined on page 52, basic undergarments, including crinoline underskirt "A" found on Plate 1, page 62.

Follow instructions carefully, covering pattern parts #1 to #5.

PATTERN PART #1: Cut out dress skirt from the black satin. Seam back and sew a 1½ inch hem at bottom; gather at top and attach to doll.

PATTERN PARTS #2, #3 AND #4: Cut out all three of the pattern parts from the black-and-white silk; sew jacket parts #2 and #3 together, leaving sufficient room for sleeves; face jacket all around with black satin at the bottom, also face front edges with same material. Seam sleeves, gather at tops, and sew into armholes; hem at bottom. Stitch a piece of black lace material to doll's neck and down front, for a dickie; attach to doll.

PATTERN PART #5: Cut out hat from the black satin, making two pieces; slip-stitch together. Fasten points one and two at mark shown in center. Tack to doll's head over one eye; sew a small bunch of tiny ostrich feathers on top of hat.

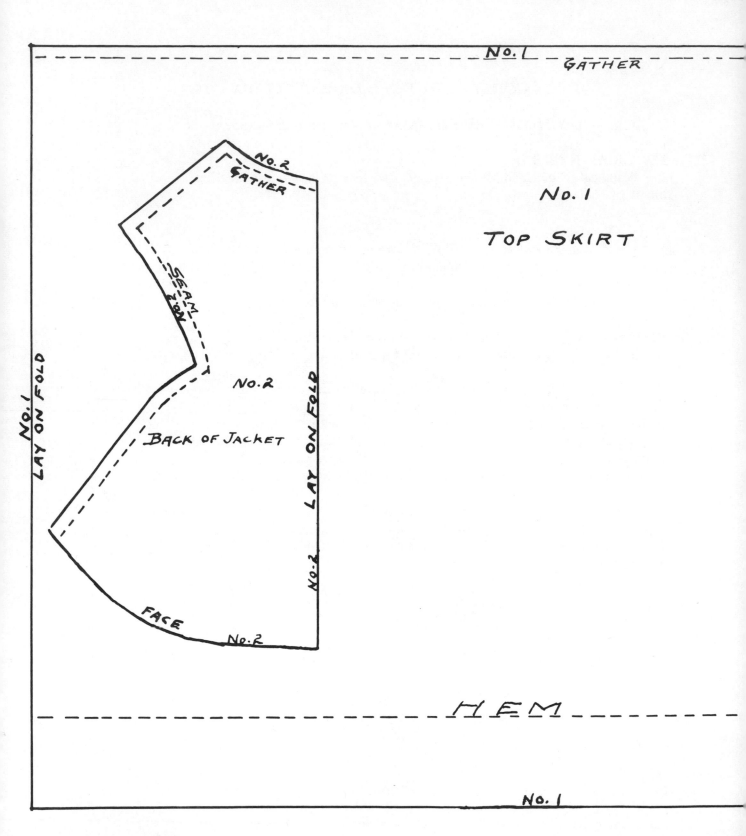

FULL SIZE

PATTERN XIV

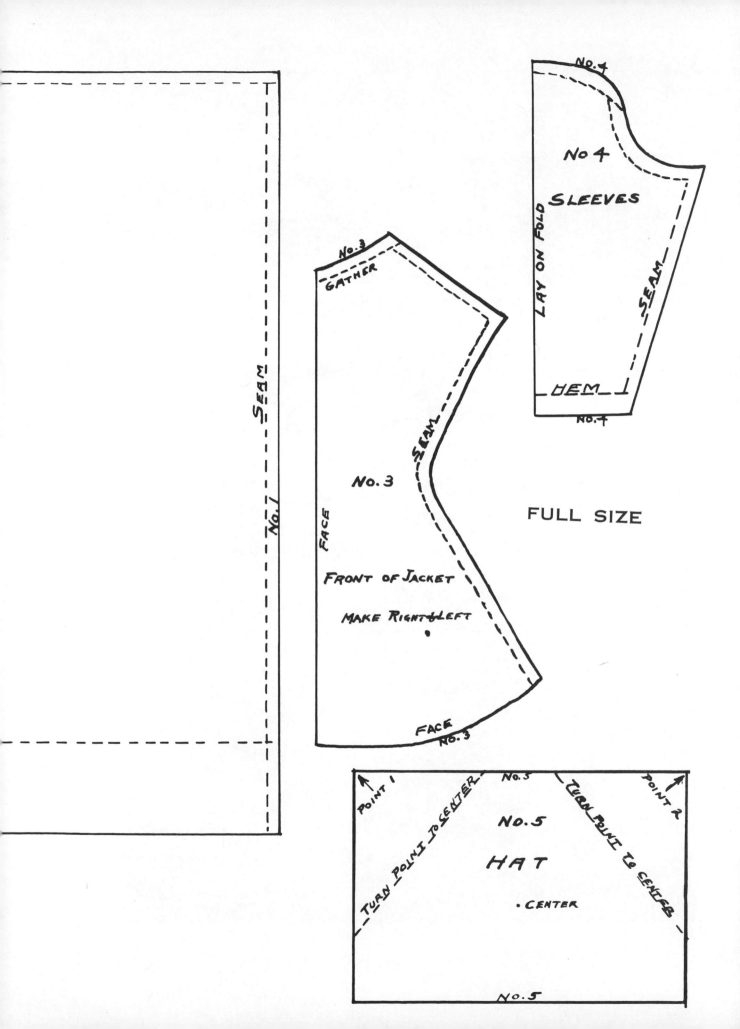

SEAM

No. 1

No. 3

GATHER

SEAM

No. 3

FACE

FRONT OF JACKET

MAKE RIGHT&LEFT

FACE

No. 3

No. 4

No 4

SLEEVES

LAY ON FOLD

SEAM

HEM

No. 4

FULL SIZE

POINT 1

No. 5

POINT 2

TURN POINT TO CENTER

TURN POINT TO CENTER

No. 5

HAT

CENTER

No. 5

CAN CAN DANCER.

MATERIAL NEEDED:
Black silk; black picot edge ruffles; pink and green baby ribbon; crystal earrings.

HOW TO MAKE:
Follow closely instructions covering pattern parts from #1 to #5.

PATTERN PARTS #1 AND #2: Cut out waist from black chiffon. Close shoulder and under arm seams; hem edges at the back; gather at neckline, and sew onto doll; finish neck with chiffon ruffle.

PATTERN PART #3: Cut out briefs from black silk; seam sides and hem leg openings; gather at top and attach to doll.

PATTERN PART #4: Cut out bustles from black silk; gather all around and pad with cotton; attach one to each side, at hips.

PATTERN PART #5: Cut out skirt from the black silk. Seam back and hem bottom; add chiffon picot ruffle around bottom; add graduated black chiffon picot ruffles in tiers, as indicated on part #5; attach to waistline; gather up front of skirt and fasten to bottom of bustle on each side.
STOCKINGS:
Make hose from fine black net, covering legs from foot to briefs. Circle legs above knees with garters of green ribbon, ornamented with pink bows.
MISCELLANEOUS ACCESSORIES:
Tie a band of black baby ribbon around neck, with bow to back. Decorate hair with dainty bows of green and pink baby ribbon.

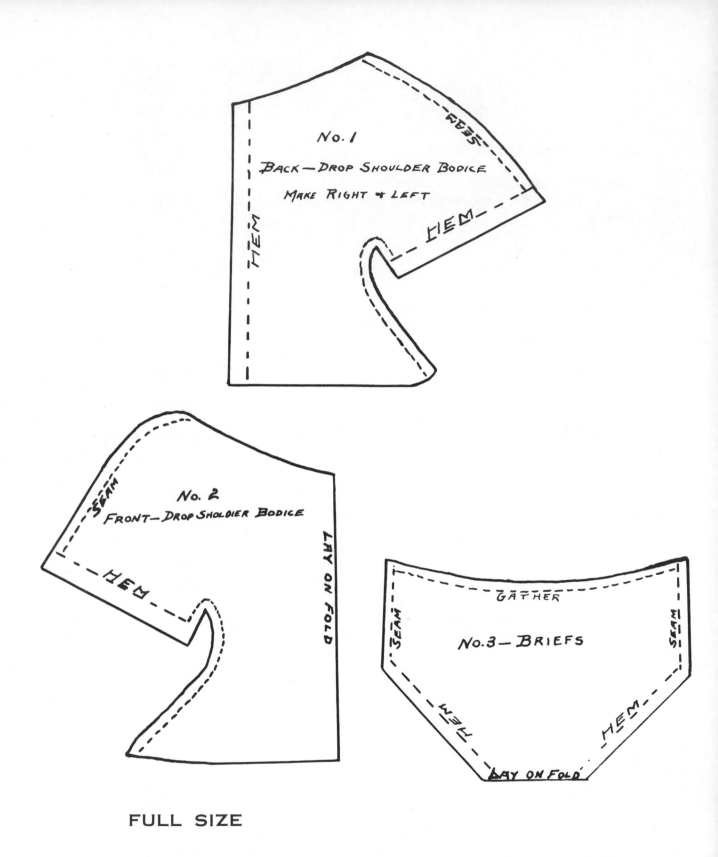

No. 1

BACK—DROP SHOULDER BODICE

MAKE RIGHT & LEFT

SEAM

HEM

HEM

No. 2

FRONT—DROP SHOLDIER BODICE

SEAM

HEM

LAY ON FOLD

GATHER

No. 3—BRIEFS

SEAM

SEAM

HEM

HEM

LAY ON FOLD

FULL SIZE

PATTERN XV

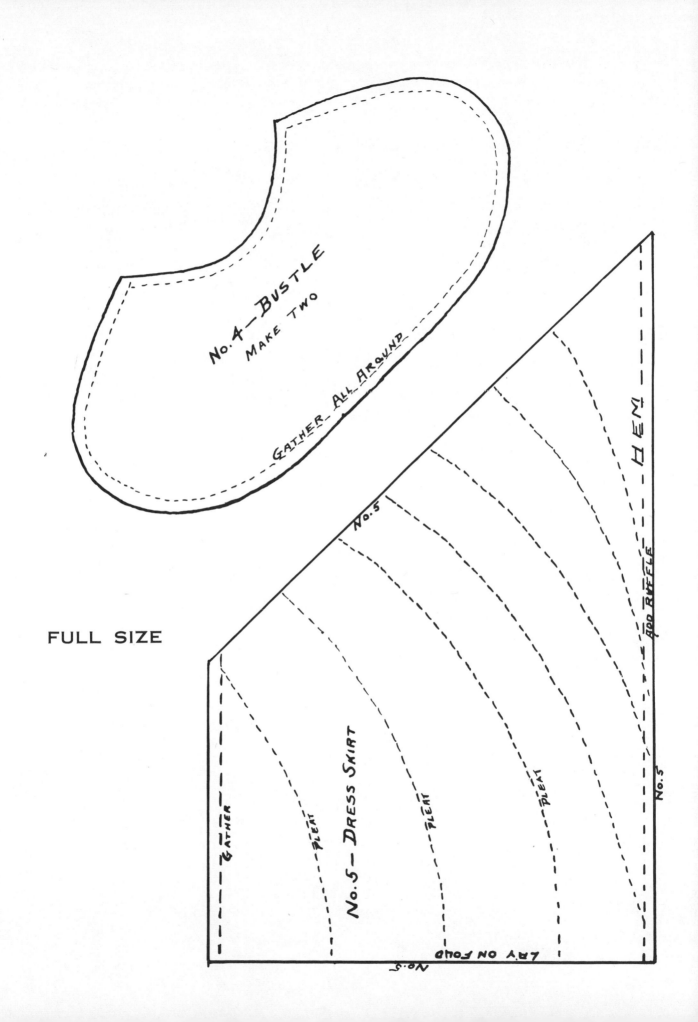

No. 4—BUSTLE
MAKE TWO

GATHER ALL AROUND

FULL SIZE

No. 5

HEM

ADD RUFFLE

No. 5

GATHER

PLEAT

No. 5—DRESS SKIRT

PLEAT

PLEAT

LAY ON FOLD

No. 5

Victorian Furniture Patterns

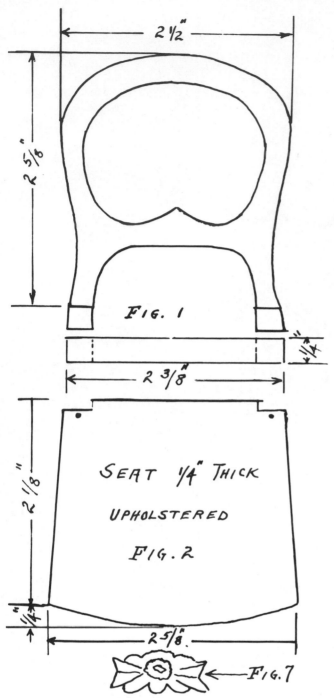

FIG. 1

2½"

2 5/8"

¼"

2 3/8"

2 1/8"

SEAT ¼" THICK

UPHOLSTERED

FIG. 2

¼"

2 5/8"

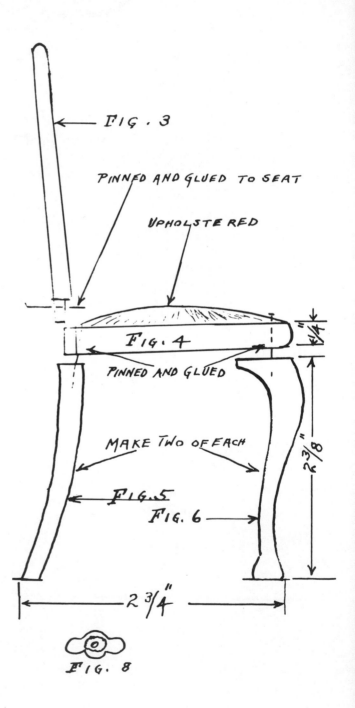

FULL SIZE

FIG. 3

PINNED AND GLUED TO SEAT

UPHOLSTERED

FIG. 4

PINNED AND GLUED

¼"

2 3/8"

MAKE TWO OF EACH

FIG. 5

FIG. 6

2 3/4"

FIG. 8

← FIG. 7

ROSEATTES ON BACK OF
CHAIR — LARGE ONE AT TOP;
SMALL ONE AT CENTER

ROSE BACK CHAIR

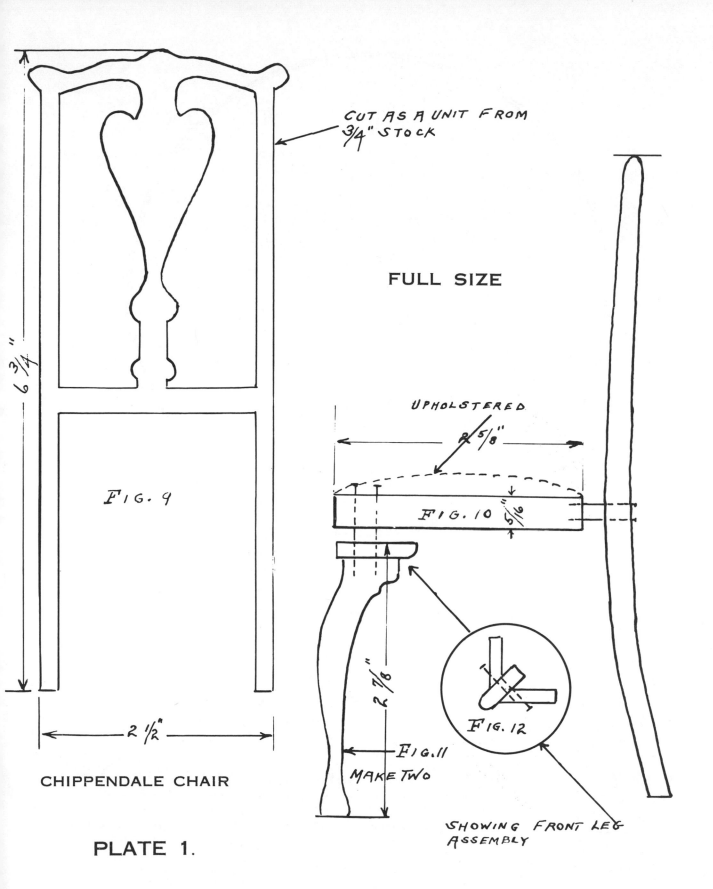

CUT AS A UNIT FROM 3/4" STOCK

FULL SIZE

UPHOLSTERED

2 5/8"

FIG. 10

5/8"

6 3/4"

FIG. 9

2 1/2"

CHIPPENDALE CHAIR

PLATE 1.

2 7/8"

FIG. 11
MAKE TWO

FIG. 12

SHOWING FRONT LEG
ASSEMBLY

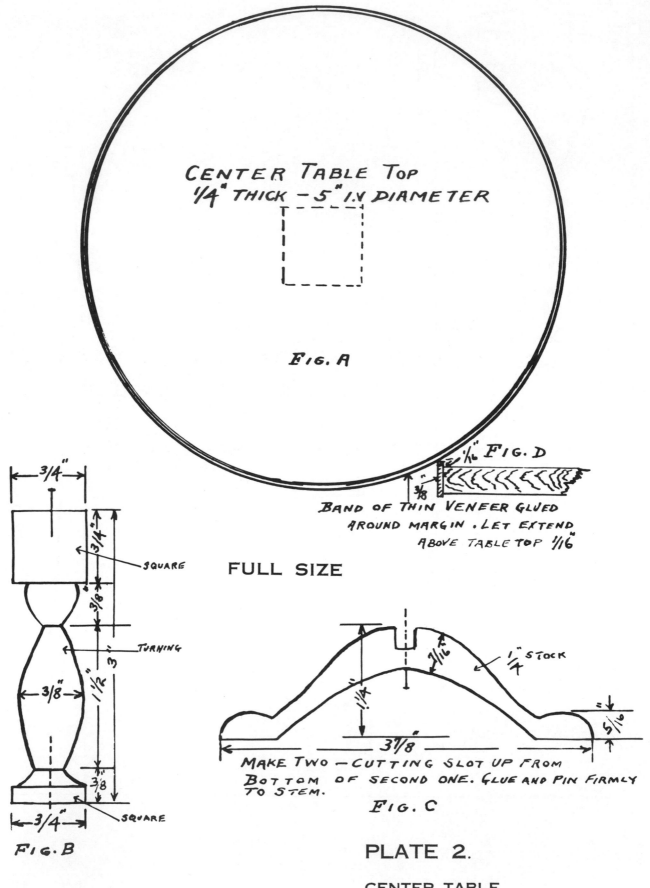

CENTER TABLE TOP
1/4" THICK — 5" IN DIAMETER

FIG. A

1/16" FIG. D

BAND OF THIN VENEER GLUED
AROUND MARGIN. LET EXTEND
ABOVE TABLE TOP 1/16"

FULL SIZE

3/4"

3/4"

SQUARE

3/8"

TURNING

3"

1 1/2"

3/8"

3/8"

3/4"

SQUARE

FIG. B

7/16"

1" STOCK

1 1/4"

3 1/8"

5/16"

MAKE TWO — CUTTING SLOT UP FROM
BOTTOM OF SECOND ONE. GLUE AND PIN FIRMLY
TO STEM.

FIG. C

PLATE 2.

CENTER TABLE

FULL SIZE

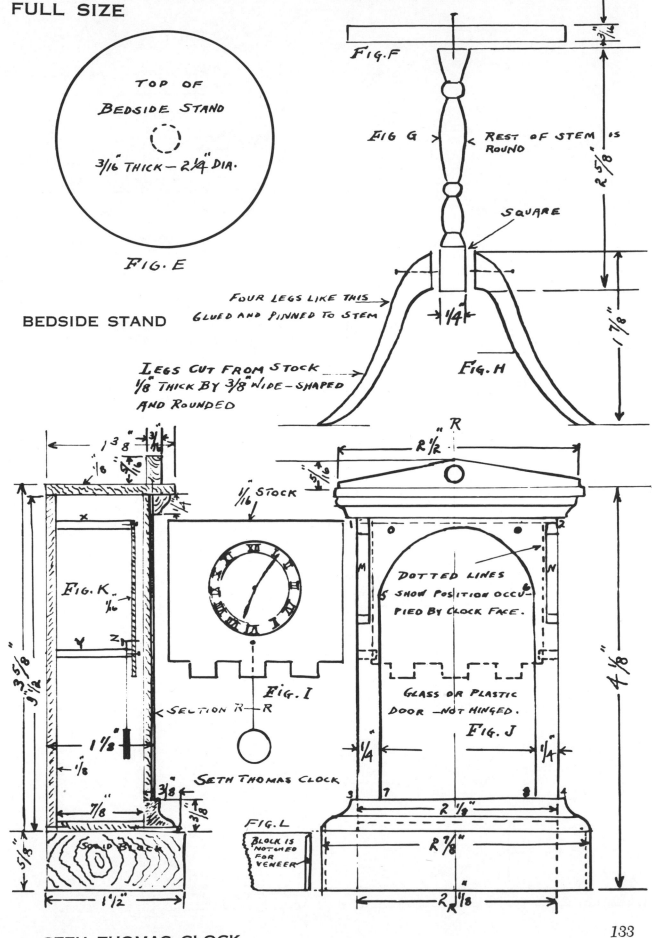

TOP OF BEDSIDE STAND
3/16" THICK — 2 1/4" DIA.

FIG. E

BEDSIDE STAND

FIG. F

FIG G → ← REST OF STEM IS ROUND

SQUARE

FOUR LEGS LIKE THIS GLUED AND PINNED TO STEM

LEGS CUT FROM STOCK 1/8" THICK BY 3/8" WIDE — SHAPED AND ROUNDED

1/4"

FIG. H

2 5/8"

1 7/8"

2 1/4"

1 3/8"   3/16"

1/8"   3/16"

1/4"

FIG. K

1/16"

3 5/8"

3 1/2"

1 1/8"

1/8"

7/8"

3/8"

3/8"

SOLID BLOCK

5/8"

1 1/2"

1/16" STOCK

SECTION R — R

FIG. I

SETH THOMAS CLOCK

FIG. L
BLOCK IS NOTCHED FOR VENEER

"R
R 1/2"

5/16"

DOTTED LINES SHOW POSITION OCCUPIED BY CLOCK FACE.

GLASS OR PLASTIC DOOR — NOT HINGED.

FIG. J

4 1/8"

1/4"   1/4"

2 1/2"

R 7/8"

2 1/8"
R

SETH THOMAS CLOCK

133

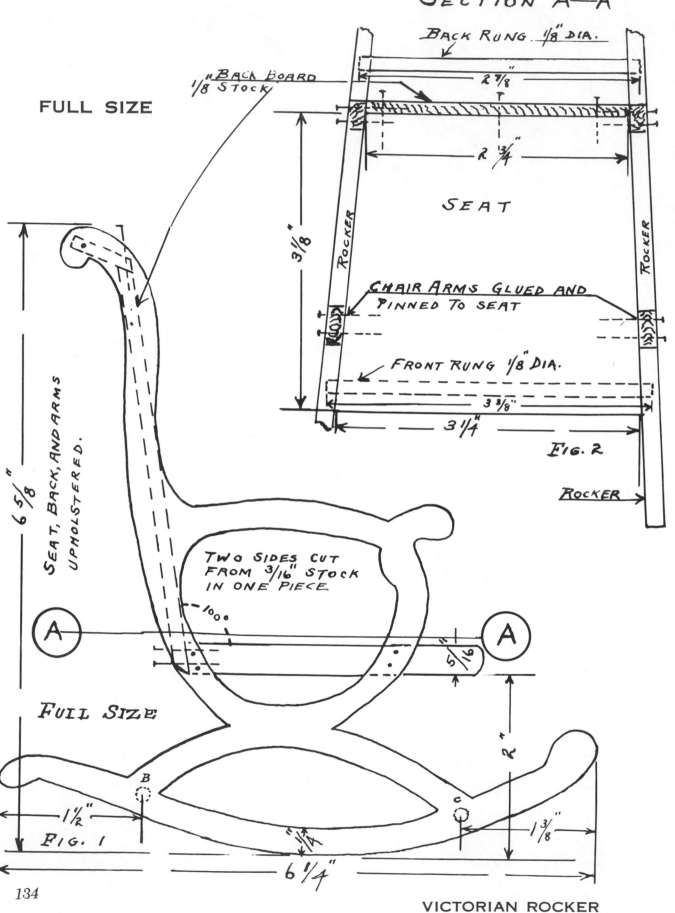

SECTION A—A

BACK RUNG. ⅛" DIA.

BACK BOARD
⅛" STOCK

FULL SIZE

2⅞"

2¾"

3⅜"

SEAT

CHAIR ARMS GLUED AND PINNED TO SEAT

FRONT RUNG ⅛" DIA.

ROCKER

ROCKER

3⅜"

3¼"

FIG. 2

ROCKER

SEAT, BACK, AND ARMS UPHOLSTERED.

6⅝"

TWO SIDES CUT FROM 3/16" STOCK IN ONE PIECE

100°

A

A

5/16"

2"

FULL SIZE

B

C

1½"

FIG. 1

¼"

1⅜"

6¼"

134

VICTORIAN ROCKER

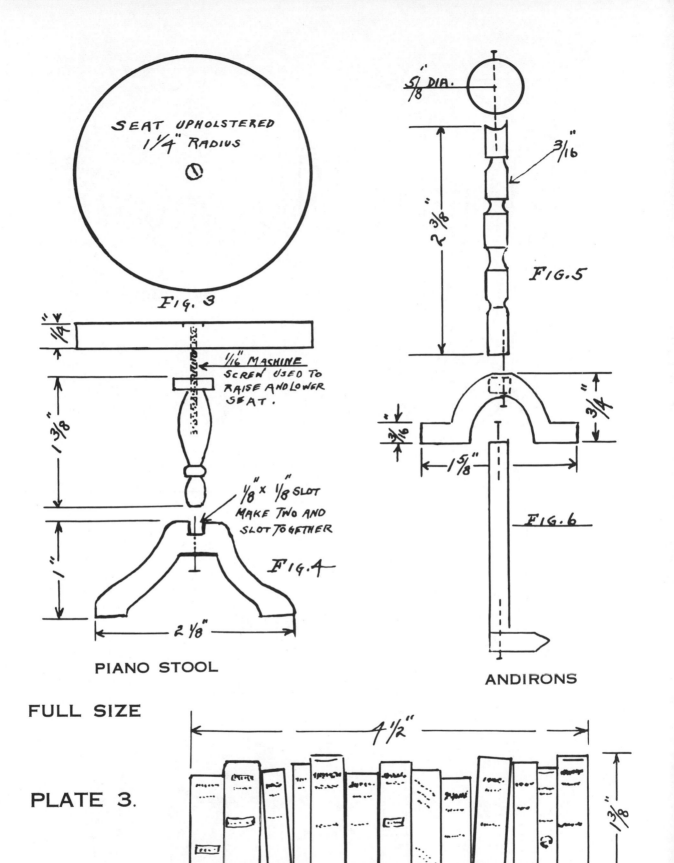

SEAT UPHOLSTERED
1¼" RADIUS

FIG. 3

5/8" DIA.

3/16"

FIG.5

2 3/8"

1/16" MACHINE SCREW USED TO RAISE AND LOWER SEAT.

¼"

1 3/8"

⅛" × ⅛" SLOT MAKE TWO AND SLOT TOGETHER

FIG.4

3/16"

3/4"

1 5/8"

FIG.6

1"

2 ⅛"

PIANO STOOL

ANDIRONS

FULL SIZE

4½"

PLATE 3.

3/8"

FIG. 7

SHELF OF BOOKS

135

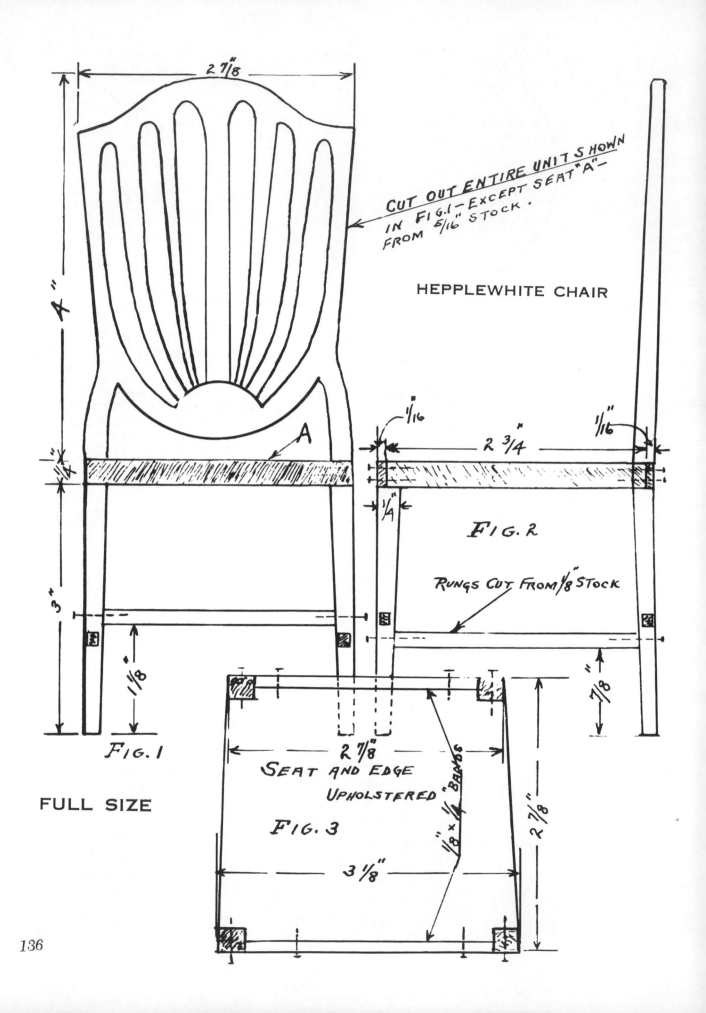

2 7/8"

CUT OUT ENTIRE UNITS SHOWN
IN FIG.1 - EXCEPT SEAT "A" -
FROM 6/16" STOCK.

HEPPLEWHITE CHAIR

4"

A

1/4"

FIG. 1

FULL SIZE

3"

1 1/8"

1/16"

2 3/4"

1/16"

1/4"

FIG. 2

RUNGS CUT FROM 1/8" STOCK

7/8"

2 7/8"

SEAT AND EDGE
UPHOLSTERED

FIG. 3

1/8 x 1/4 "BANDS

2 7/8"

3 1/8"

136

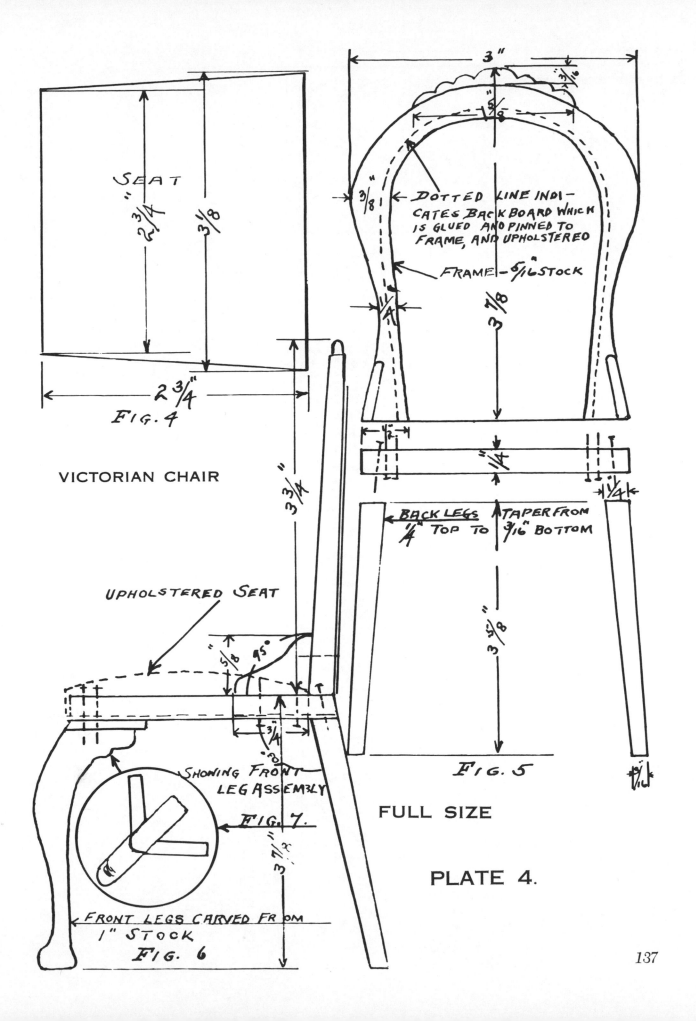

SEAT

2 3/4"

3/8"

2 3/4"

FIG. 4

VICTORIAN CHAIR

UPHOLSTERED SEAT

3 3/4"

5/8"

95°

3/4"

SHOWING FRONT
LEG ASSEMBLY

FIG. 7.

3 7/8"

FRONT LEGS CARVED FROM
1" STOCK

FIG. 6

3"

3/16"

5/8"

DOTTED LINE INDI-
CATES BACK BOARD WHICH
IS GLUED AND PINNED TO
FRAME, AND UPHOLSTERED

FRAME—5/16" STOCK

3/8"

3/8"

1/4"

1/4"

1/2"

1/4"

1/4"

BACK LEGS TAPER FROM
1/4" TOP TO 3/16" BOTTOM

3 5/8"

3/16"

FIG. 5

FULL SIZE

PLATE 4.

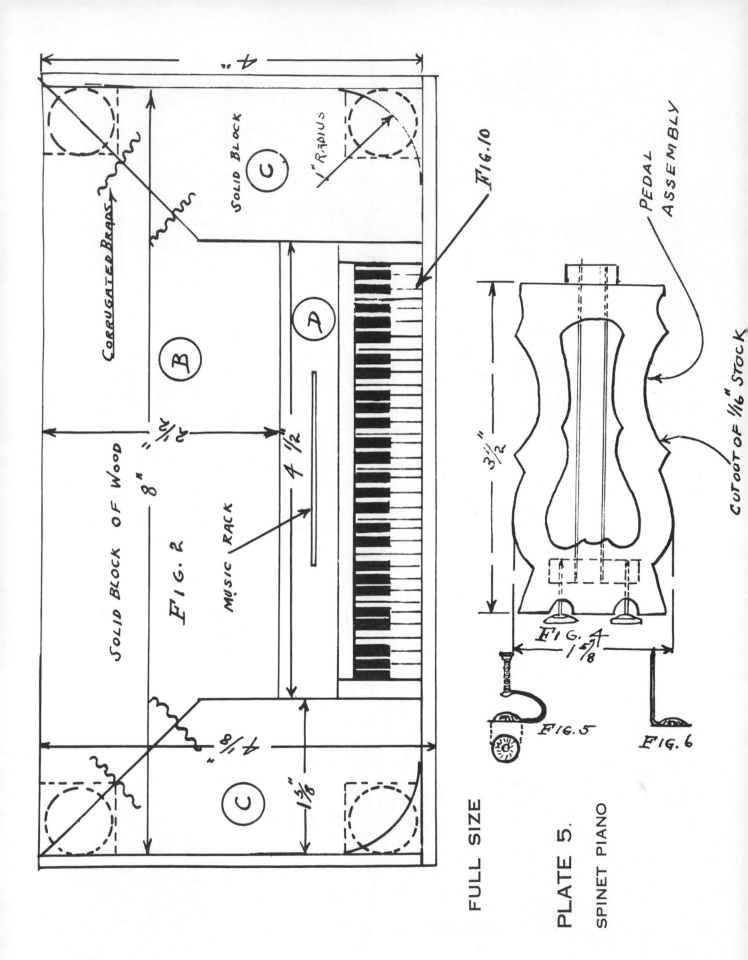

CORRUGATED BRADS

SOLID BLOCK

C

1" RADIUS

FIG. 10

B

SOLID BLOCK OF WOOD

8"

2½"

A

4½"

FIG. 2

MUSIC RACK

C

4⅛"

1⅞"

4"

PEDAL ASSEMBLY

3½"

CUTOUT OF 1/16" STOCK

FIG. 4

1⅛"

FIG. 5

FIG. 6

FULL SIZE

PLATE 5.

SPINET PIANO

138

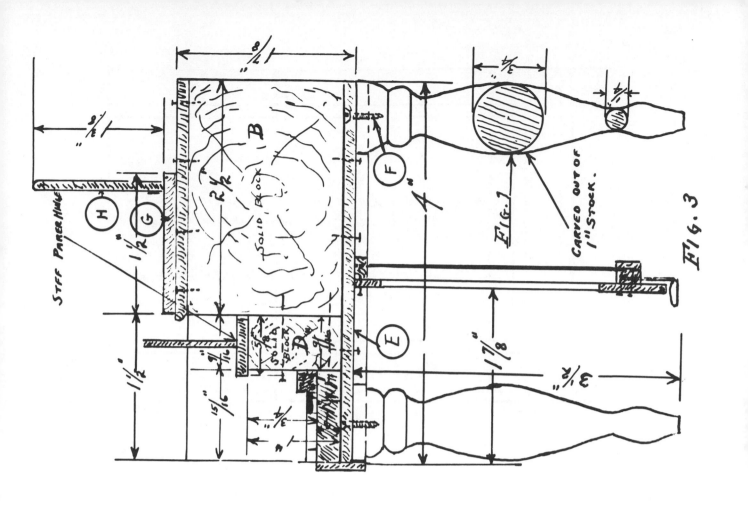

FIG. 3

FIG. 1

CARVED OUT OF 1" STOCK.

B

SOLID BLOCK

2½"

STIFF PAPER HINGE

H

G

1½"

1½"

15/16"

¾"

SOLID BLOCK

F

E

4"

1⅞"

3½"

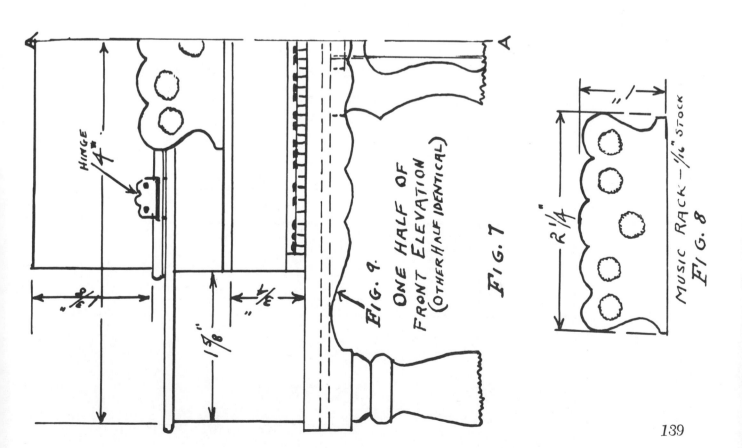

HINGE

4"

FIG. 9

ONE HALF OF FRONT ELEVATION
(OTHER HALF IDENTICAL)

FIG. 7

1½"

3/4"

1⅞"

A

MUSIC RACK—1/16" STOCK
FIG. 8

1"

2¼"

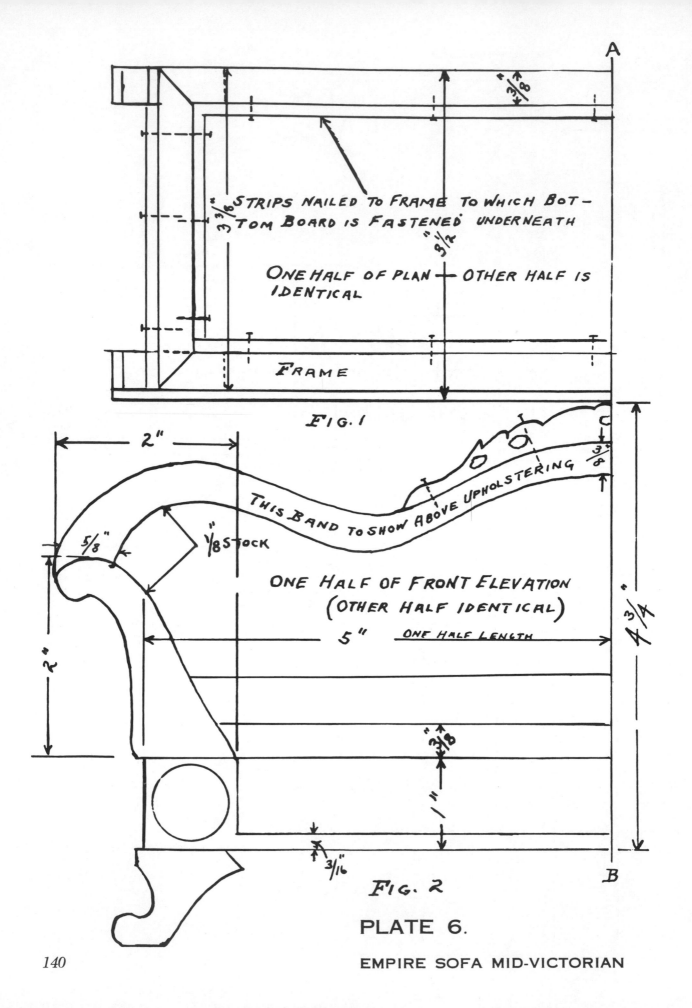

A

STRIPS NAILED TO FRAME TO WHICH BOT-
TOM BOARD IS FASTENED UNDERNEATH

3/8"

3/2"

ONE HALF OF PLAN — OTHER HALF IS
IDENTICAL

FRAME

FIG. 1

2"

THIS BAND TO SHOW ABOVE UPHOLSTERING

3/8"

5/8"   1/8 STOCK

ONE HALF OF FRONT ELEVATION
(OTHER HALF IDENTICAL)

2"   5"   ONE HALF LENGTH

4 3/4"

3/8"

1"

3/16"

FIG. 2

B

PLATE 6.

140   EMPIRE SOFA MID-VICTORIAN

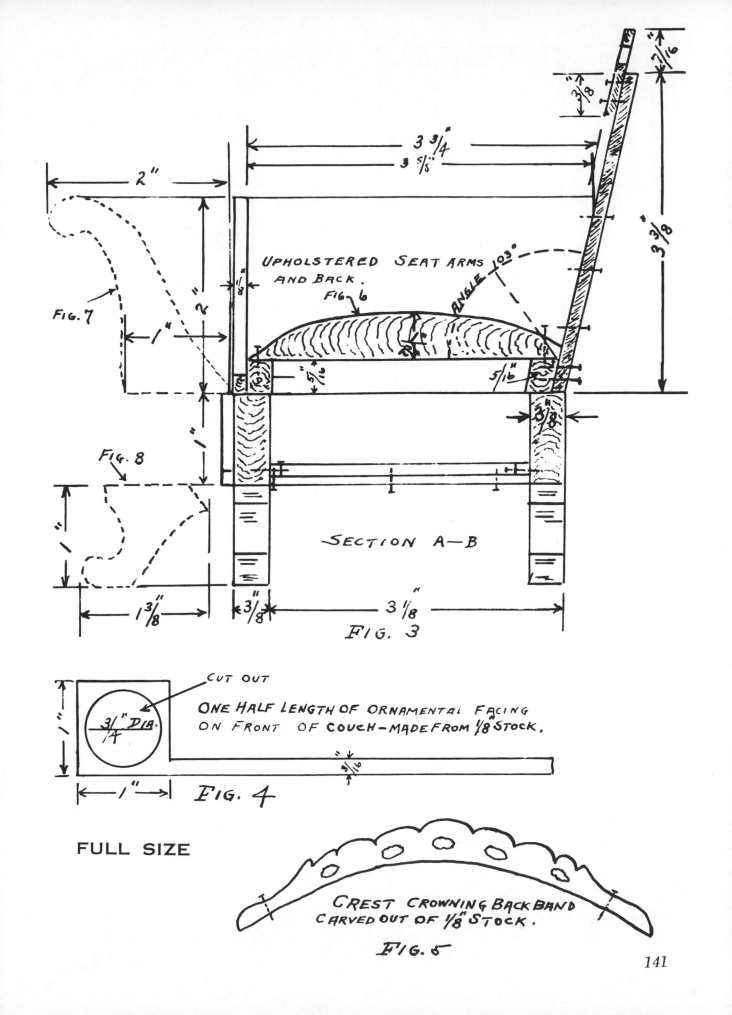

2"

3 3/4"

3 5/8"

7/16"

3/8"

3 3/8"

Upholstered Seat Arms and Back.
Fig. 6

Angle 103°

Fig. 7

1/8"

2"

1"

5/16"

5/16"

3/8"

1"

Fig. 8

1"

SECTION A—B

1 3/8"

3/8"

3 1/8"

FIG. 3

CUT OUT

ONE HALF LENGTH OF ORNAMENTAL FACING
ON FRONT OF COUCH—MADE FROM 1/8" STOCK.

3/4" DIA.

1"

1"

3/16"

FIG. 4

FULL SIZE

CREST CROWNING BACK BAND
CARVED OUT OF 1/8" STOCK.

FIG. 5

141

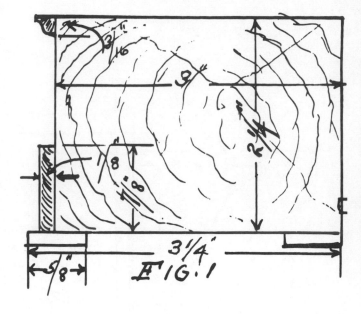

3/16

9

2 1/4

8
1/8

5/8

3 1/4

FIG. 1

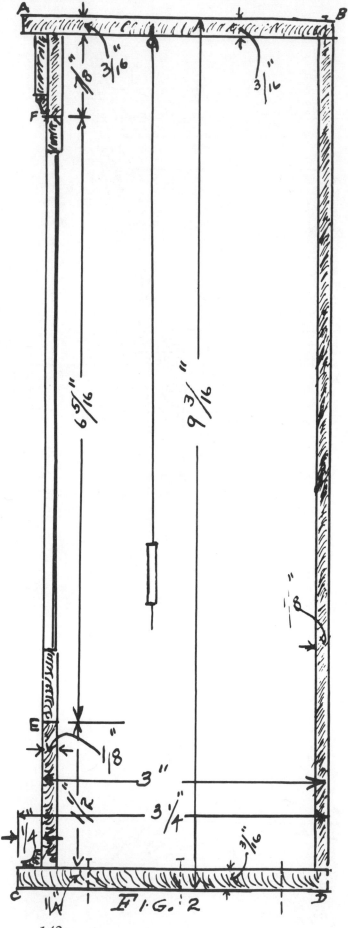

A · · · · · · B

1/8 3/16

3/16

F

6 5/16

9 3/16

E

1/8

3 "

1 1/2

3 1/4

1/4

3/16

1 "

C · · · · D

FIG. 2

142

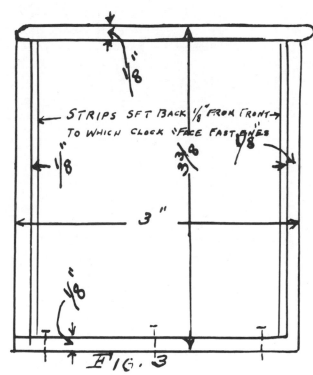

1/8

STRIPS SET BACK 1/8" FROM FRONT
TO WHICH CLOCK FACE FASTENES

1/8

1/8

3/8

3 "

1/8

1/8

FIG. 3

FULL SIZE

PLATE 7.

GRANDFATHERS' CLOCK

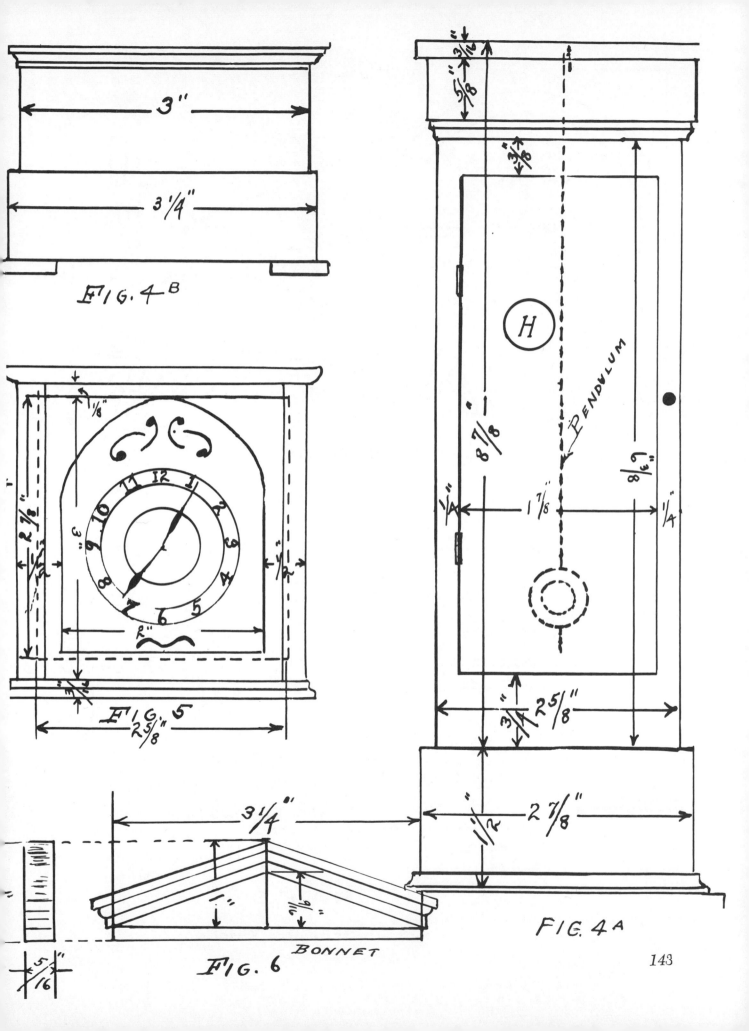

FIG. 4 B

FIG. 5

2 5/8"

BONNET

FIG. 6

3 1/4"

5/16"

FIG. 4 A

PENDULUM

H

143

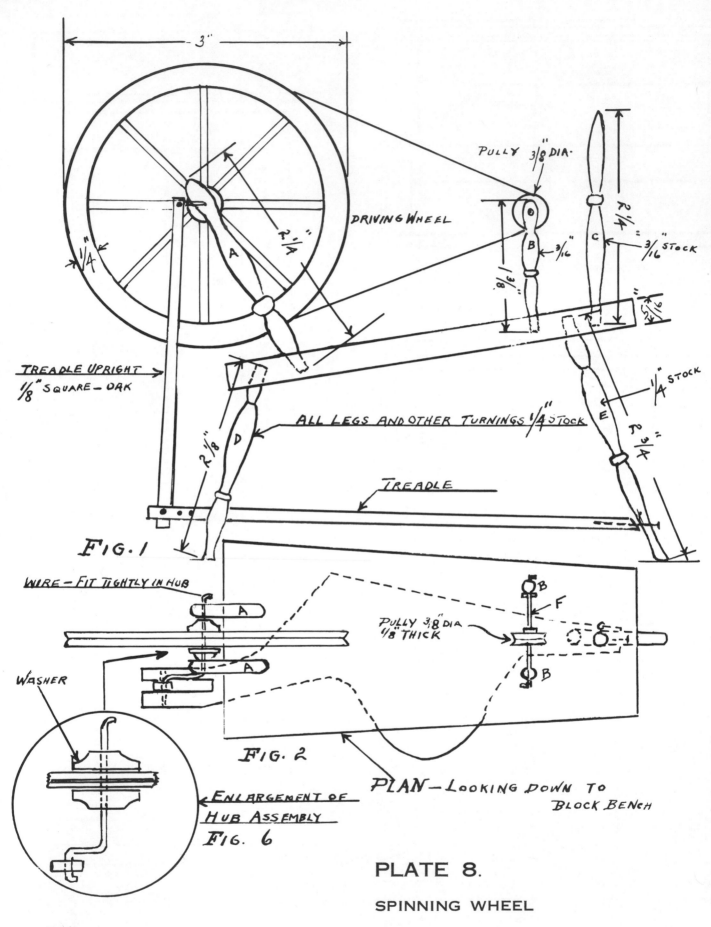

3"

PULLY 3/8" DIA.

DRIVING WHEEL

3/16"

3/16" STOCK

2 1/4"

8 1/8"

A

2 3/4"

TREADLE UPRIGHT
1/8" SQUARE — OAK

ALL LEGS AND OTHER TURNINGS 1/4" STOCK

1/4" STOCK

E

2 3/4"

2 1/8"

D

TREADLE

FIG. 1

WIRE — FIT TIGHTLY IN HUB

A

B

PULLY 3/8" DIA.
1/8" THICK

F

C

A

B

WASHER

FIG. 2

ENLARGEMENT OF
HUB ASSEMBLY
FIG. 6

PLAN — LOOKING DOWN TO
BLOCK BENCH

PLATE 8.

SPINNING WHEEL

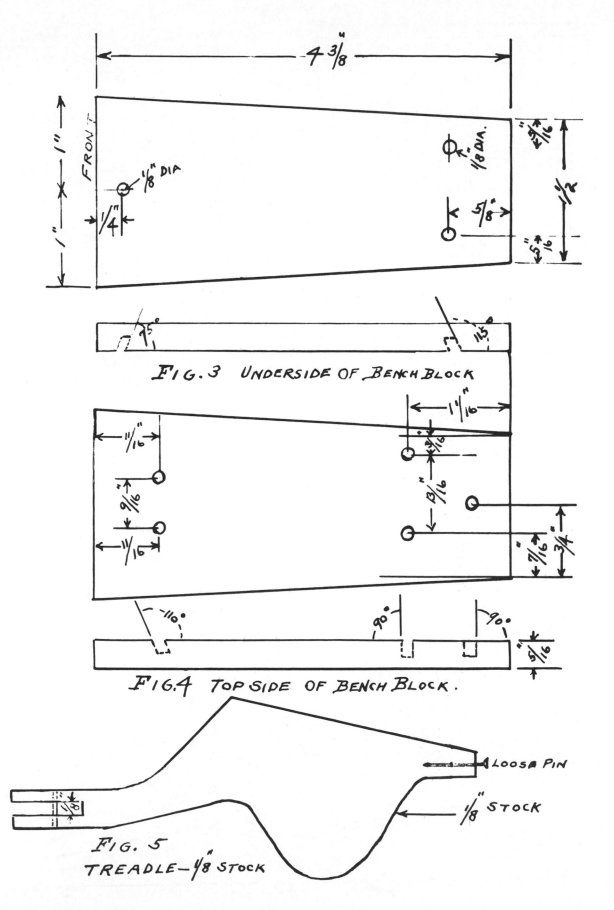

4 3/8"

FRONT

1"

1"

1/8" DIA

1/4"

1/8" DIA.

5/8"

3/16"

1/2"

5/16"

75°

115°

FIG. 3   UNDERSIDE OF BENCH BLOCK

1 1/16"

11/16"

9/16"

11/16"

3/16"

13/16"

7/16"

3/4"

110°

90°

90°

5/16"

FIG. 4   TOP SIDE OF BENCH BLOCK.

LOOSE PIN

1/8" STOCK

1/8"

FIG. 5
TREADLE—1/8" STOCK

FULL SIZE   UNLESS OTHERWISE INDICATED

145

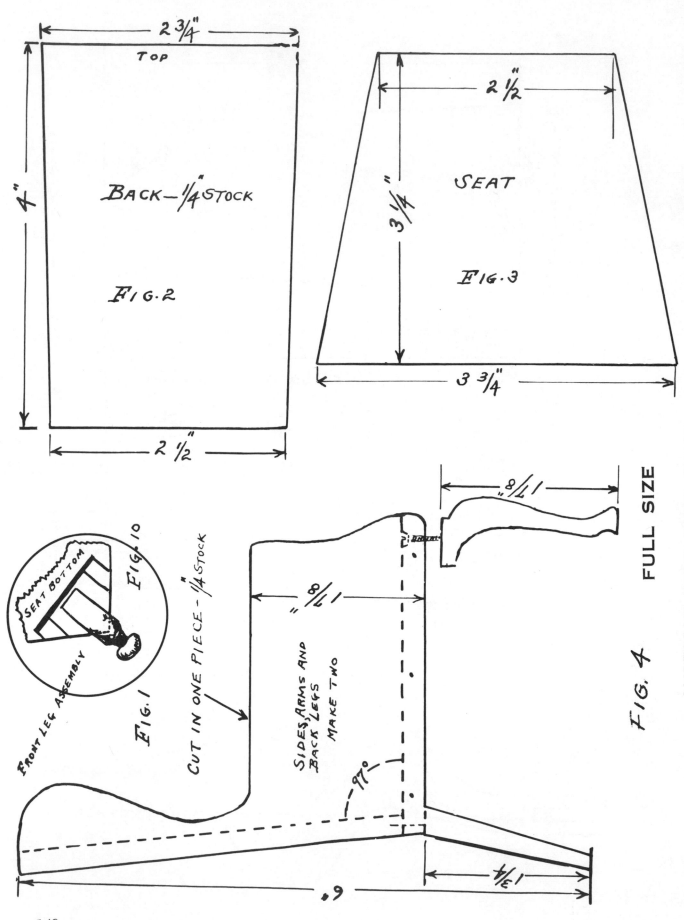

2 3/4"

TOP

BACK—1/4" STOCK

FIG. 2

4"

2 1/2"

2 1/2"

SEAT

FIG. 3

3 1/4"

3 3/4"

FRONT LEG ASSEMBLY

SEAT BOTTOM

FIG. 10

FIG. 1

CUT IN ONE PIECE — 1/4" STOCK

SIDES, ARMS AND BACK LEGS MAKE TWO

1 7/8"

1 7/8"

97°

6"

1 3/4"

FIG. 4   FULL SIZE

AMERICAN WING BACK CHAIR

146

PLATE 9.

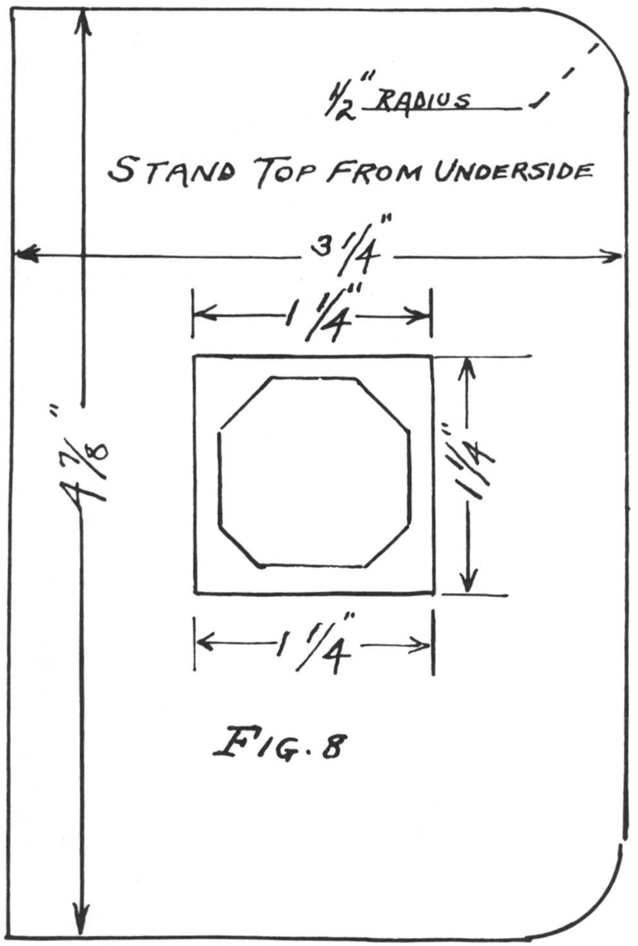

1/2" RADIUS
STAND TOP FROM UNDERSIDE
3 1/4"
1 1/4"
1 1/4"
1 1/4"
4 7/8"
FIG. 8

FULL SIZE

COLONIAL HIGH BACK WALL STAND

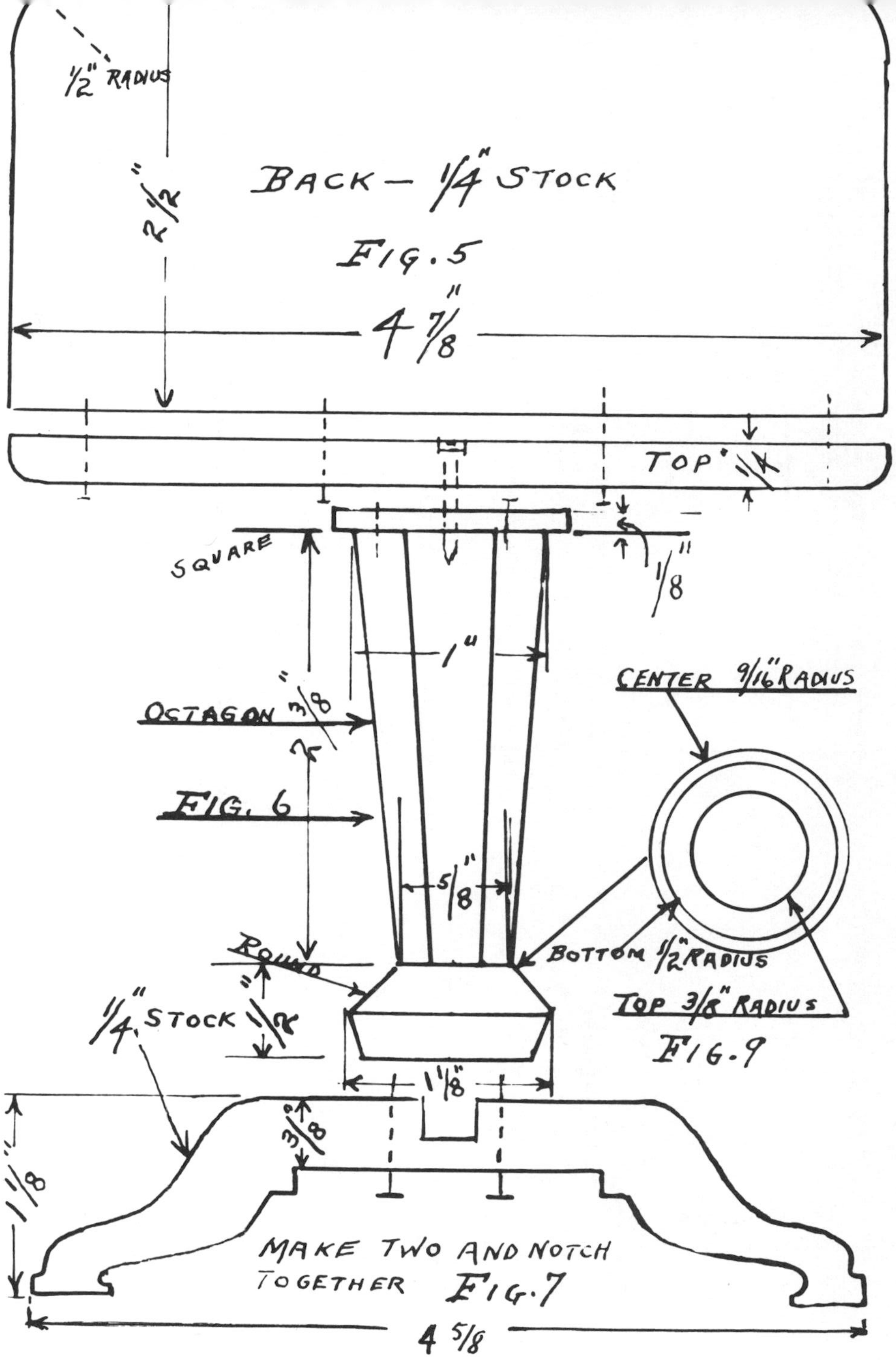

1/2" RADIUS
BACK — 1/4" STOCK
FIG. 5
2 1/2"
4 7/8"
TOP 1/4"
1/8"
SQUARE
1"
OCTAGON 3/8"
FIG. 6
5/8"
ROUND
1/4" STOCK
1/2"
1 1/8"
CENTER 9/16" RADIUS
BOTTOM 1/2" RADIUS
TOP 3/8" RADIUS
FIG. 9
3/8"
1 1/8"
MAKE TWO AND NOTCH TOGETHER
FIG. 7
4 5/8

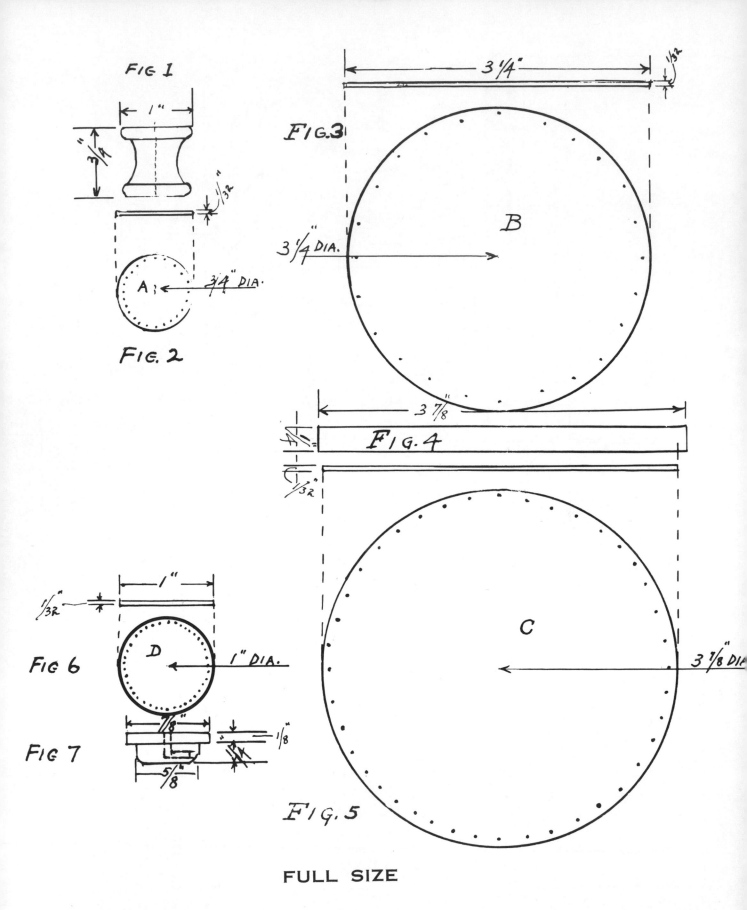

FIG 1

FIG. 2

A

3/4" DIA.

FIG.3

B

3 1/4"

1/32

3 1/4" DIA.

FIG.4

3 7/8"

1/32

1/32

C

3 7/8" DIA

FIG 6

D

1" DIA.

1"

1/32"

FIG 7

1/8"

5/8"

3/8"

FIG. 5

FULL SIZE

148

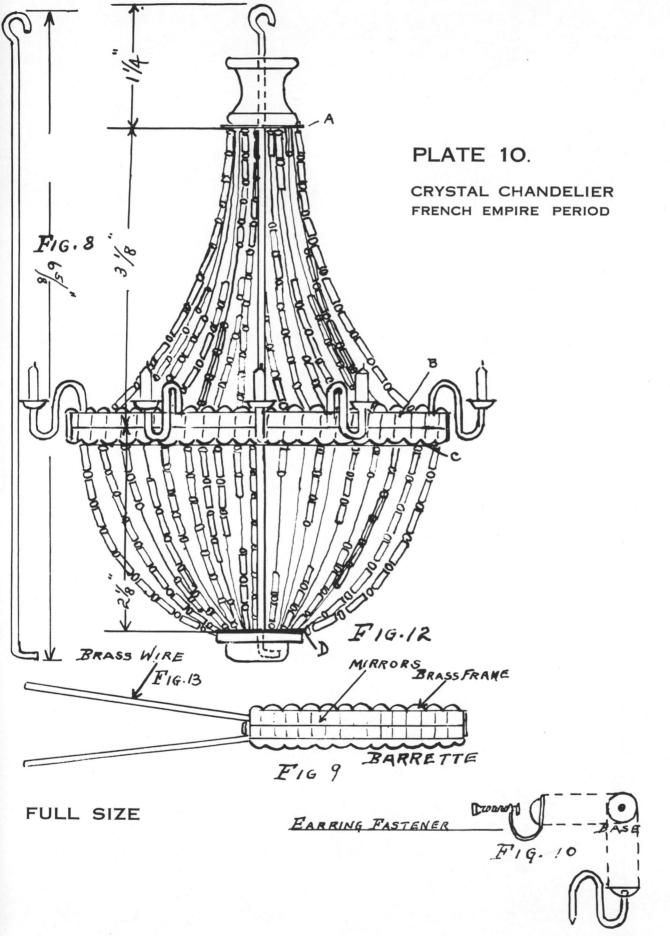

PLATE 10.

CRYSTAL CHANDELIER
FRENCH EMPIRE PERIOD

FIG. 8

1¼"

3⅜"

5⅝"

2⅝"

A

B

C

D

FIG. 12

BRASS WIRE
FIG. 13

MIRRORS
BRASS FRAME

BARRETTE

FIG 9

FULL SIZE

EARRING FASTENER

BASE

FIG. 10

CANDELABRA FIG. 11

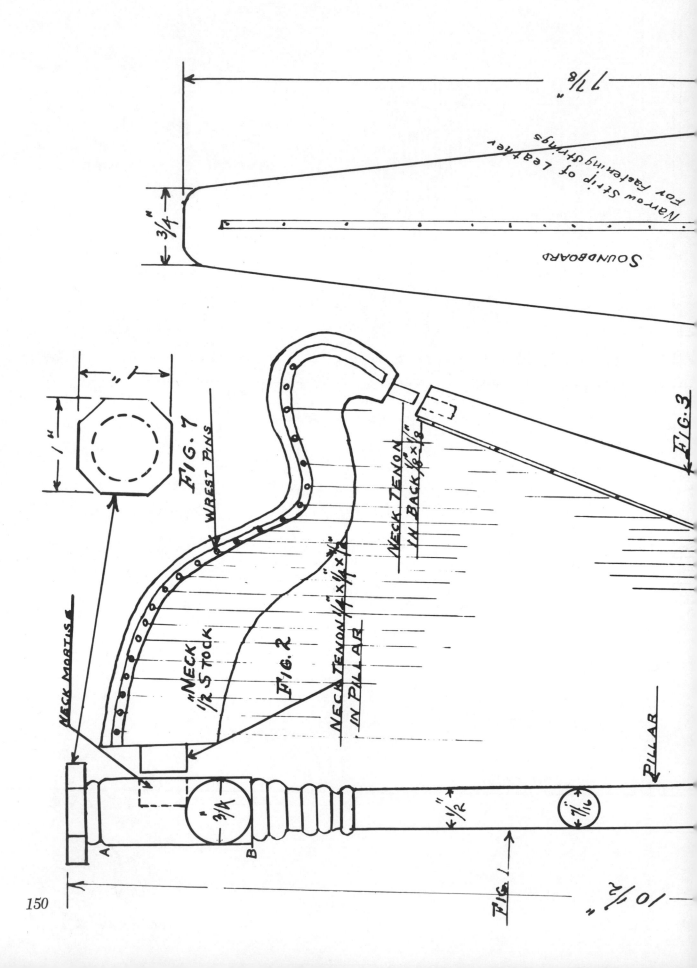

SOUNDBOARD

Narrow Strip of Leather
For Fastening Strings

7⅛"

¾"

FIG. 3

FIG. 7

WREST PINS

NECK MORTISE

NECK
½ STOCK

FIG. 2

NECK TENON ¼"×¼"×½"
IN PILLAR

NECK TENON ½"×⅝"
IN BACK

PILLAR

½"

¾"

1½"

A   B

FIG. 1

10½"

1"

1"

150

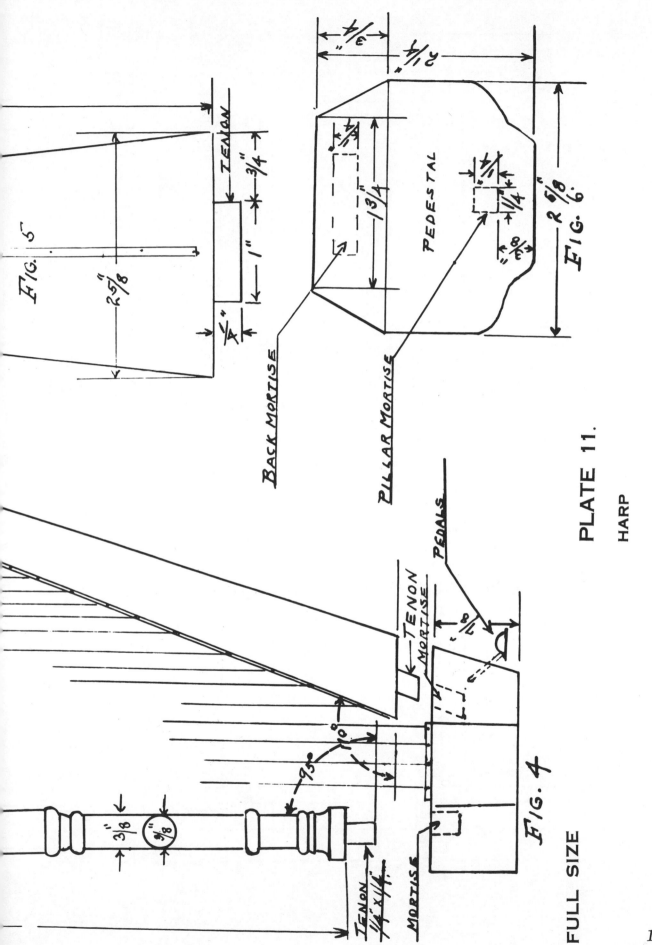

FIG. 5

FIG. 6.

PEDESTAL

BACK MORTISE

PILLAR MORTISE

TENON ¼"×¼"

MORTISE

TENON

MORTISE

PEDALS

FIG. 4

FULL SIZE

PLATE 11.

HARP

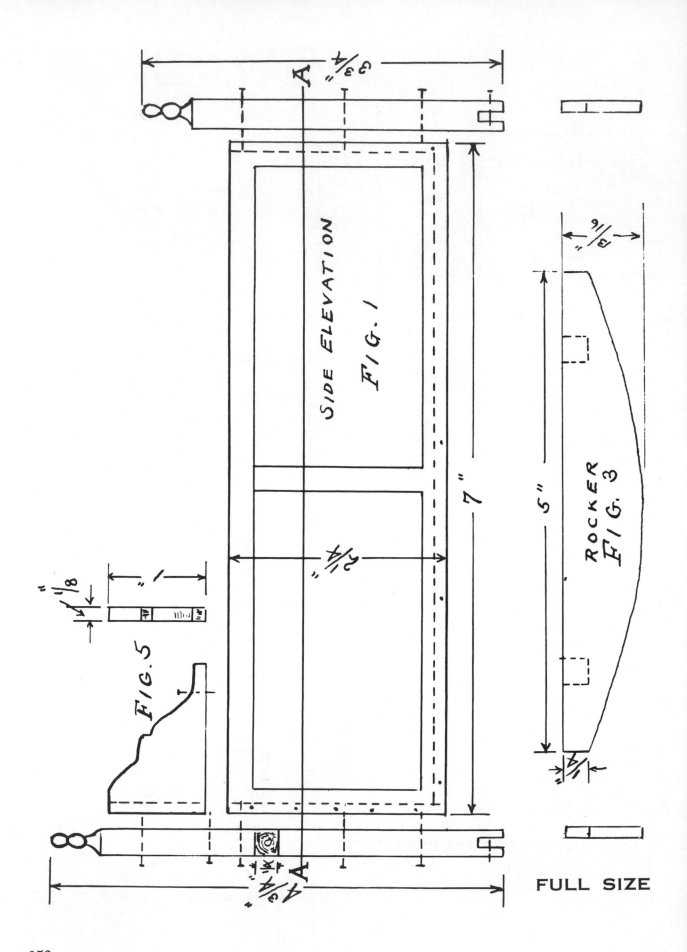

SIDE ELEVATION
FIG. 1

ROCKER
FIG. 3

FIG. 5

FULL SIZE

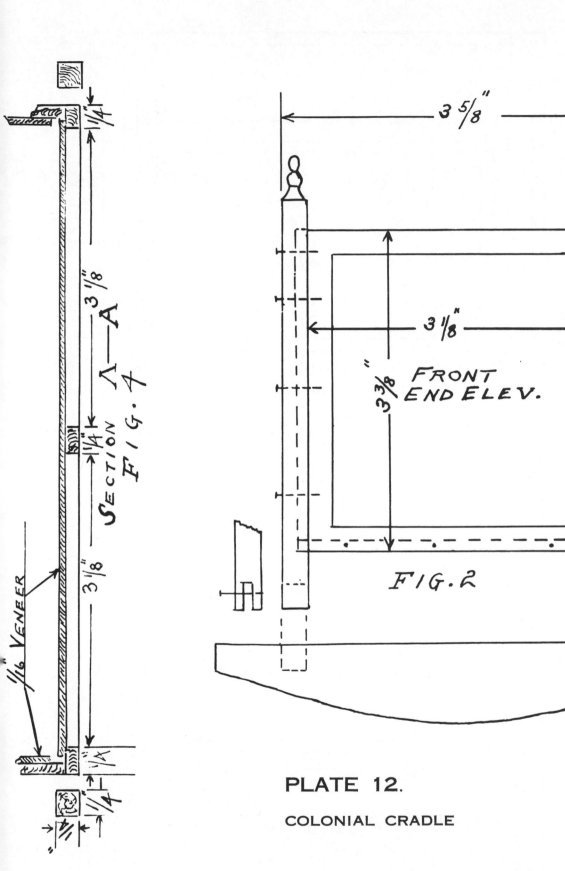

1/4"

3 1/8"

Section A—A

FIG. 4

1 1/4"

3 1/8"

1/16" Veneer

1/4"

1/4"

1/4"

3 5/8"

3 1/8"

3 3/8"

FRONT
END ELEV.

FIG. 2

PLATE 12.

COLONIAL CRADLE

153

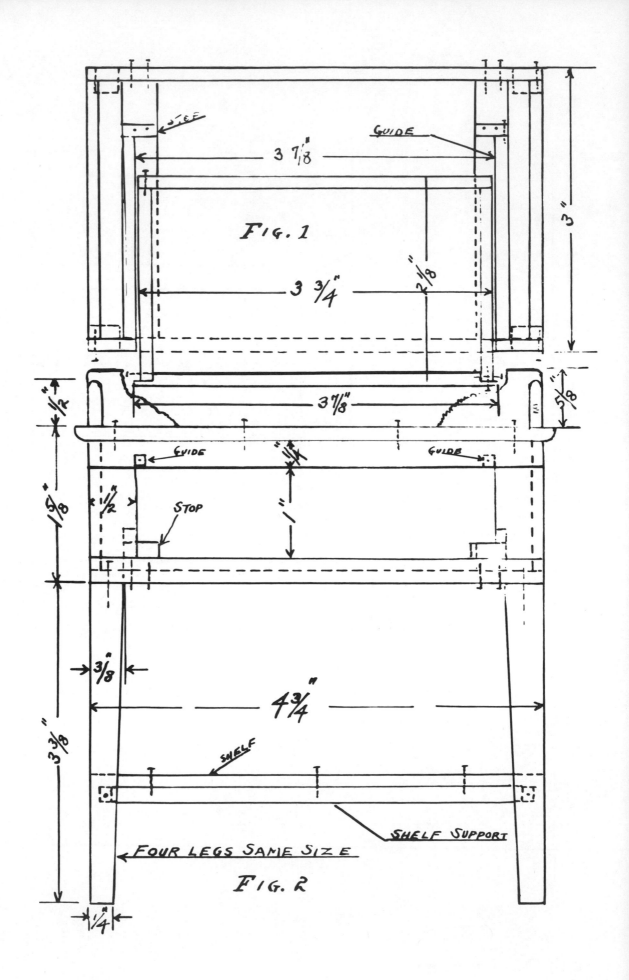

FIG. 1

FIG. 2

FOUR LEGS SAME SIZE

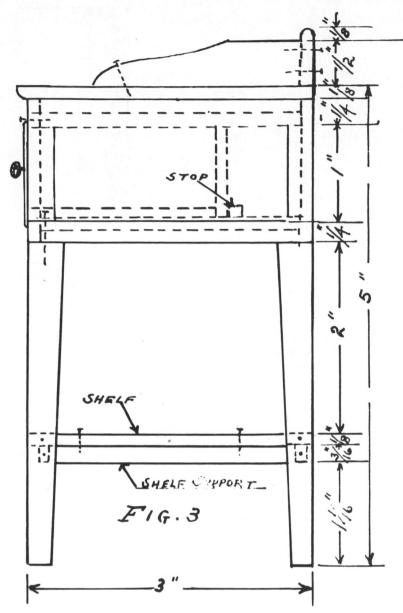

FULL SIZE

STOP

SHELF

SHELF SUPPORT

FIG. 3

1/8"
1/2"
1/8"
1/4"
1"
1/4"
2"
5"
3/16"
3/8"
1/16"

3"

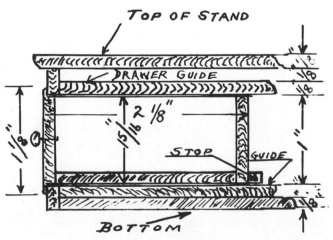

TOP OF STAND

DRAWER GUIDE

2 1/8"

15/16"

STOP

GUIDE

BOTTOM

1/8"
1/8"
1/8"
1/8"
1/8"

SECTION THRU DRAWER
FIG. 4

PLATE 13.

WASH STAND
EARLY AMERICAN

155

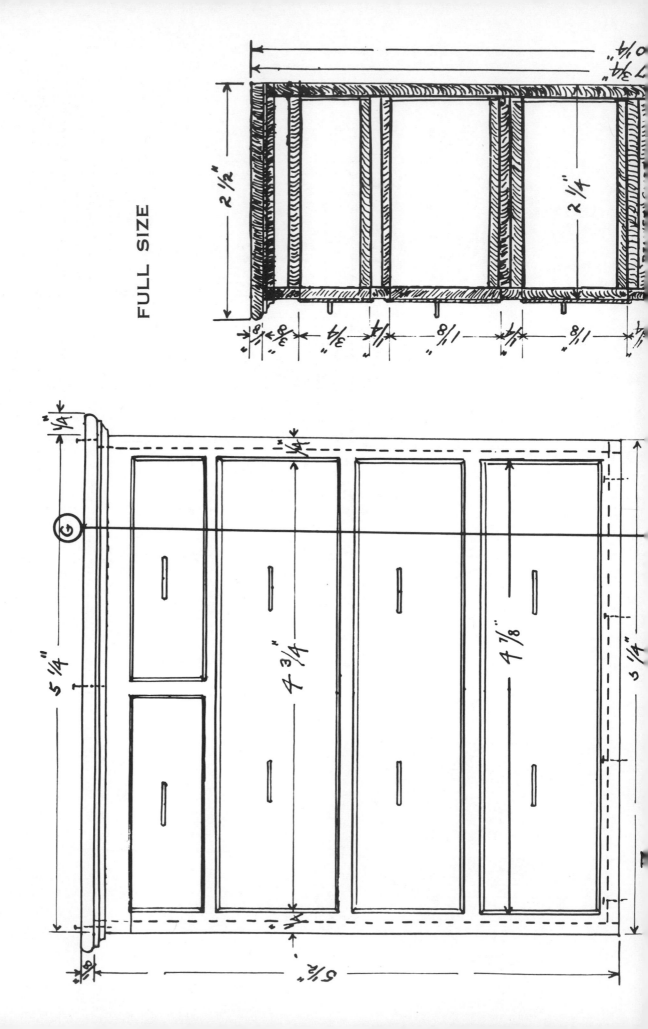

FULL SIZE

2 1/2"

2 1/4"

1/8" 3/8" 3/4" 1/4" 1/8" 1/4" 1/8" 1/4"

1 3/4"
6 1/4"

1/4"

1/4"

4 3/4"

4 7/8"

5 1/4"

5 1/4"

G

1/8"

5 1/2"

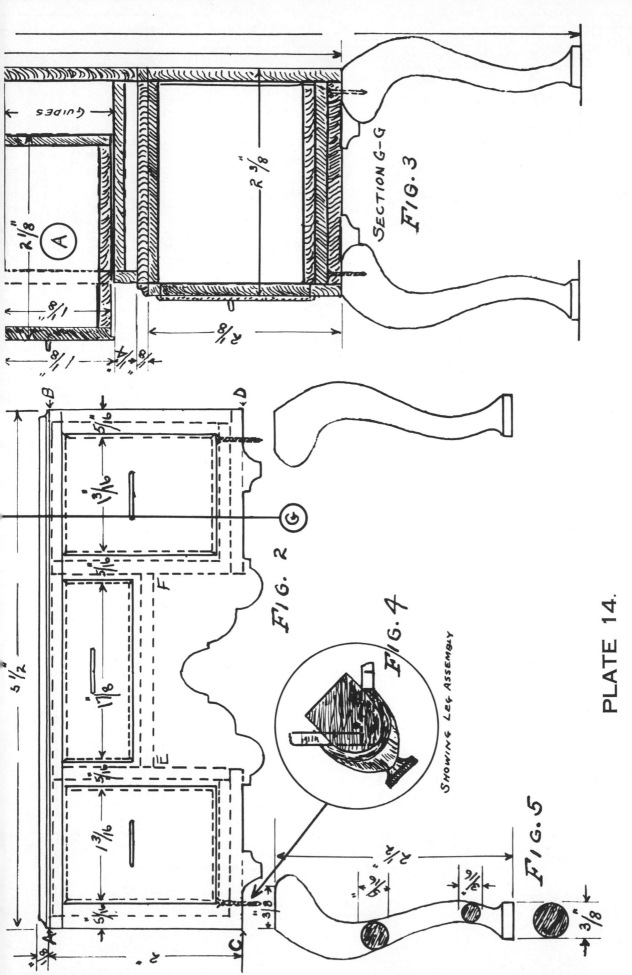

GUIDES

2 1/8"

A

1 1/8"

1 1/8"

1/4"

1/8"

2 3/8"

2 1/8"

SECTION G-G
FIG. 3

B

5/16"

3/16"

5/16"

F

5 1/2"

1 1/8"

E

5/16"

G

FIG. 2

3/16"

5/16"

2"

C

3/8"

FIG. 4

SHOWING LEG ASSEMBLY

2 1/2"

3/16"

3/16"

3/8"

FIG. 5

PLATE 14.

AMERICAN HIGHBOY 1780

157

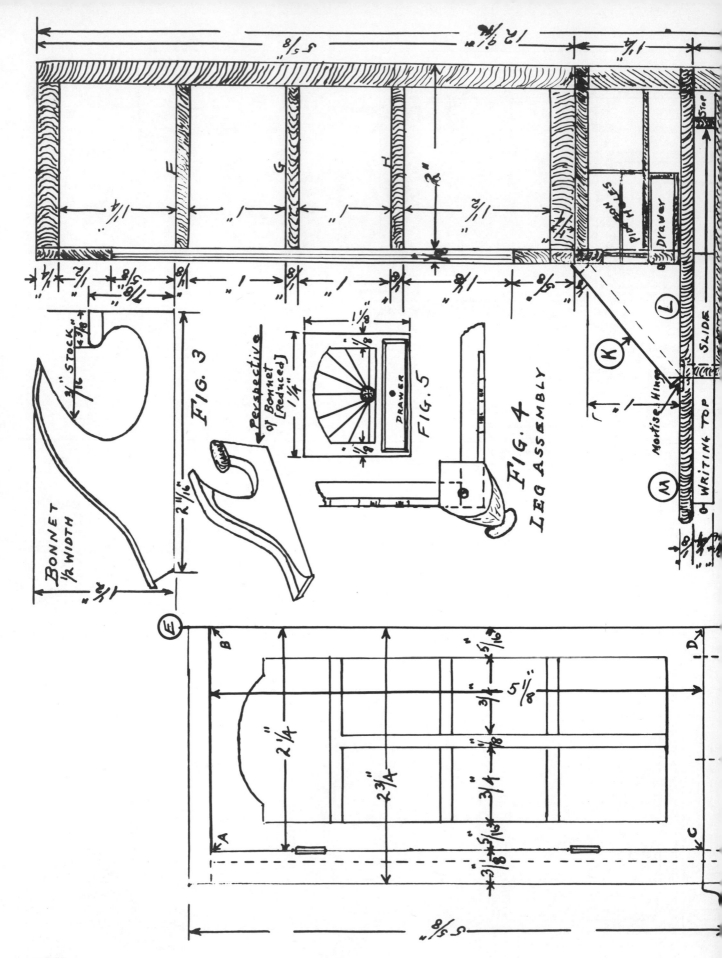

FIG. 3

BONNET ½ WIDTH

3" STOCK

2 11/16"

1 ½"

Perspective
of Bonnet
[Reduced]

1 ⅛"

1 ¼"

DRAWER

FIG. 5

FIG. 4
LEG ASSEMBLY

PIN HOLES

DRAWER

STOP

L

K

M

WRITING TOP

SLIDE

Mortise Hinge

1"

E

B

2 ¼"

2 ¾"

5 ⅛"

11/16"

3/4"

⅛"

3/4"

5/16"

⅜"

A

C

D

5 ⅝"

12 ¾"

5 ⅝"

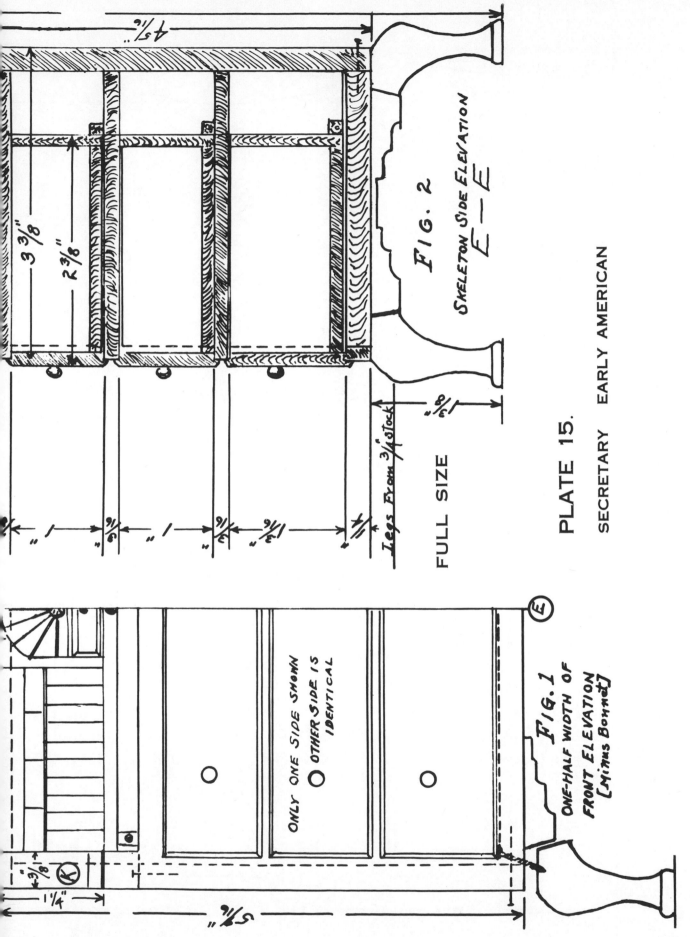

4 5/16"

3 3/8"

2 3/8"

FIG. 2

SKELETON SIDE ELEVATION
E—E

1 3/8"

Legs From 3/4 Stock

FULL SIZE

PLATE 15.

SECRETARY   EARLY AMERICAN

1"   9/16"   1"   9/16"   1 3/8"   1 1/4"

ONLY ONE SIDE SHOWN
O OTHER SIDE IS
IDENTICAL

FIG. 1

ONE-HALF WIDTH OF
FRONT ELEVATION
[MINUS BONNET]

3 3/8"

K

1 1/4"

5 1/2"

E

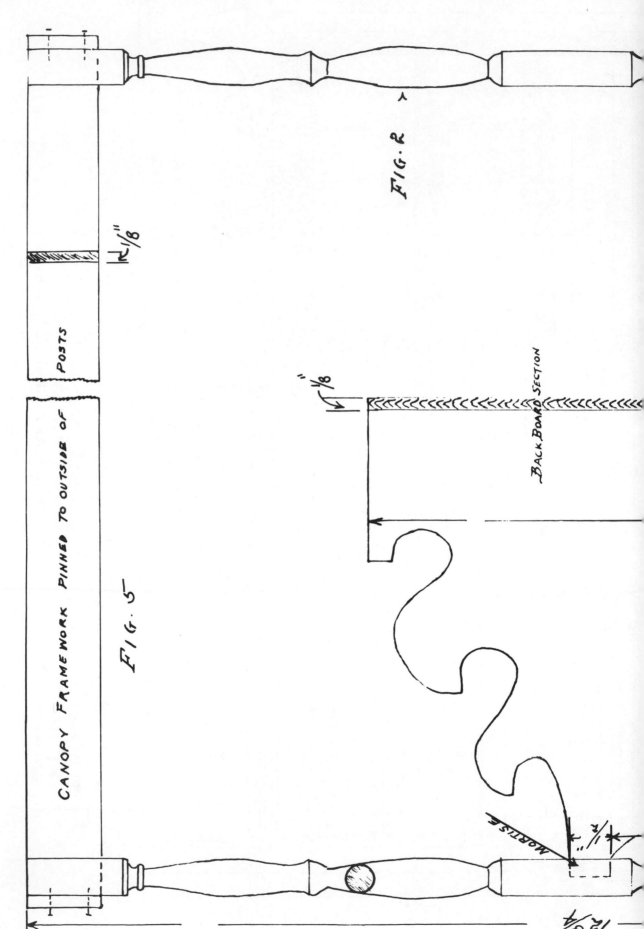

POSTS

⟵ ⅛"

FIG. 2

CANOPY FRAMEWORK PINNED TO OUTSIDE OF

FIG. 5

⅛"

BACK BOARD SECTION

MORTISE

½"

1"

12¾"

160

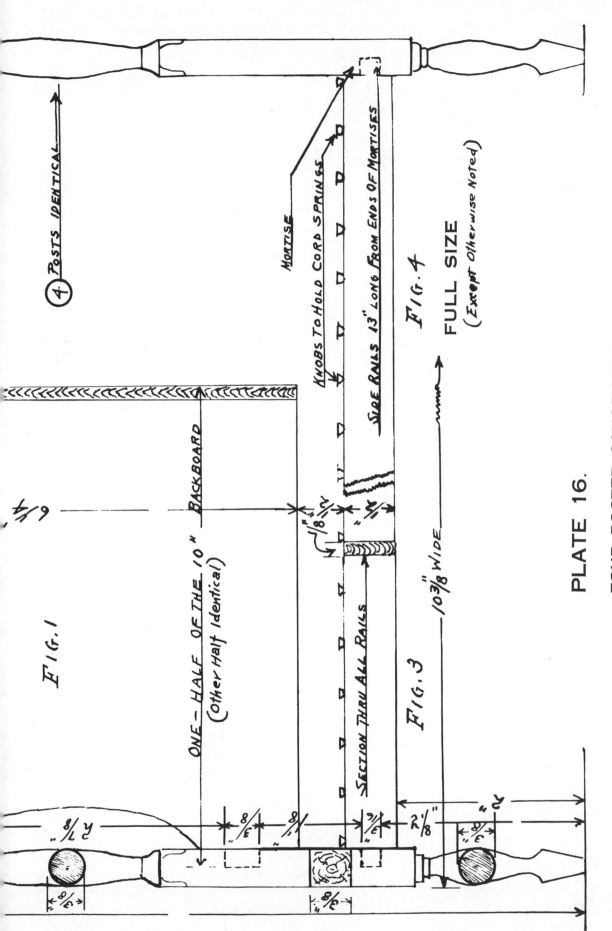

4 POSTS IDENTICAL

FIG. 1

ONE-HALF OF THE 10" BACKBOARD
(Other Half Identical)

MORTISE

KNOBS TO HOLD CORD SPRINGS

SIDE RAILS 13" LONG FROM ENDS OF MORTISES

SECTION THRU ALL RAILS

FIG. 3

FIG. 4

FULL SIZE
(Except Otherwise Noted)

6 1/4"

1 1/8"

1/2"

10 3/8" WIDE

2 7/8"

3/4"

3/4"

1 1/8"

3 1/2"

2 1/8"

3/4"

2 1/2"

1/2"

PLATE 16.

FOUR POSTER CANOPY BED 1800

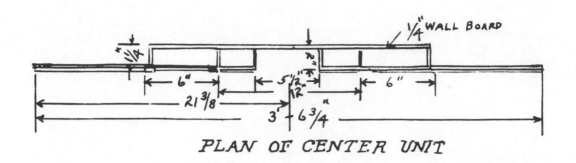

PLAN OF CENTER UNIT

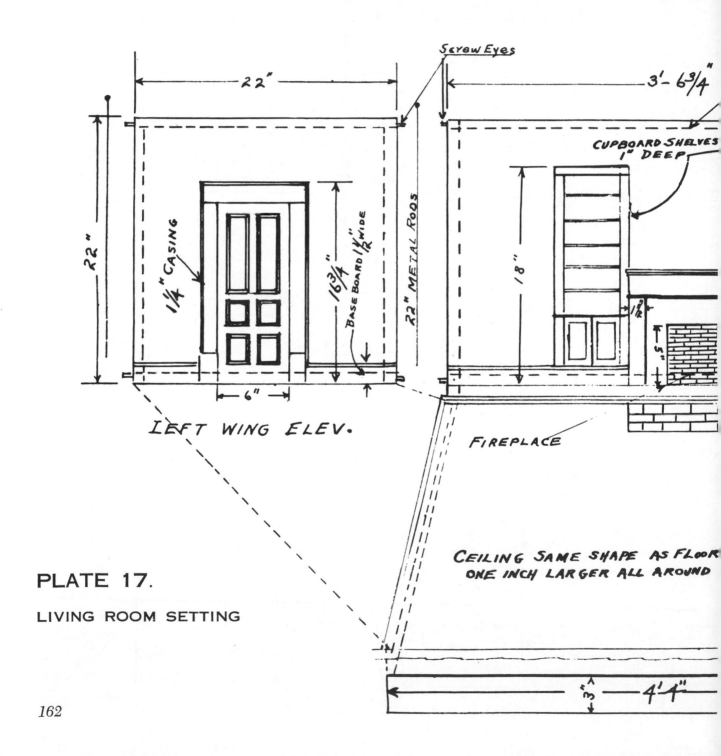

PLATE 17.

LIVING ROOM SETTING

162

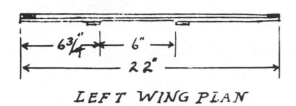

LEFT WING PLAN

RIGHT WING PLAN

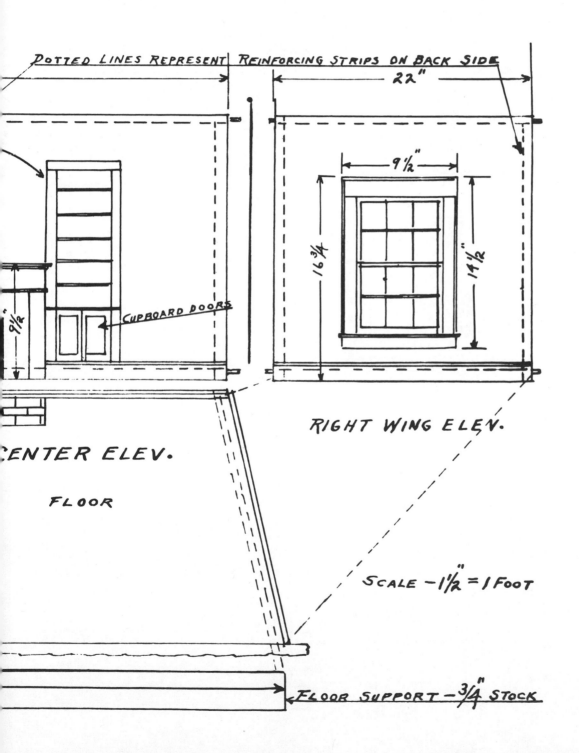

DOTTED LINES REPRESENT REINFORCING STRIPS ON BACK SIDE

22"

9½"

16¾

14½

CUPBOARD DOORS

CENTER ELEV.

FLOOR

RIGHT WING ELEV.

SCALE — 1½" = 1 FOOT

FLOOR SUPPORT — ¾" STOCK

163

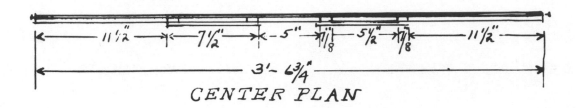

CENTER PLAN

11½" 7½" 5" 1⅛" 5½" ⅞" 11½"

3'- 6¾"

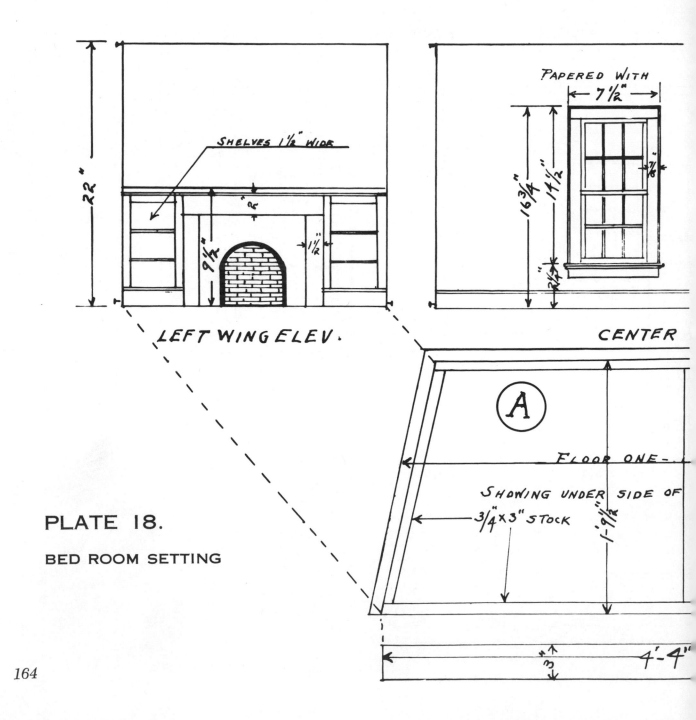

SHELVES 1½" WIDE

22"

2"

9½"

1½"

LEFT WING ELEV.

PAPERED WITH

7½"

16¾"

14½"

⅞"

2½"

CENTER

PLATE 18.

BED ROOM SETTING

A

FLOOR ONE—

SHOWING UNDER SIDE OF

¾"x3" STOCK

1'-9½"

3"

4'-4"

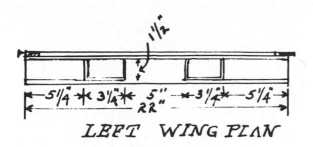

LEFT WING PLAN

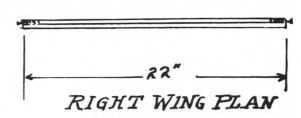

RIGHT WING PLAN

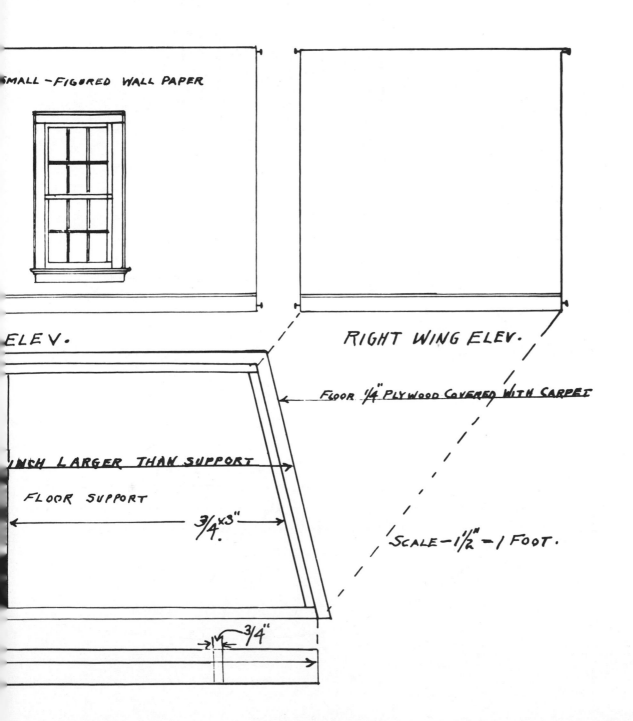

SMALL-FIGURED WALL PAPER

ELEV.

RIGHT WING ELEV.

FLOOR 1/4" PLYWOOD COVERED WITH CARPET

INCH LARGER THAN SUPPORT

FLOOR SUPPORT

3/4"x3".

SCALE—1 1/2" = 1 FOOT.

1" 3/4"

5 1/4" 3 1/4" 5" 3 1/4" 5 1/4"
22"

1 1/2"

22"

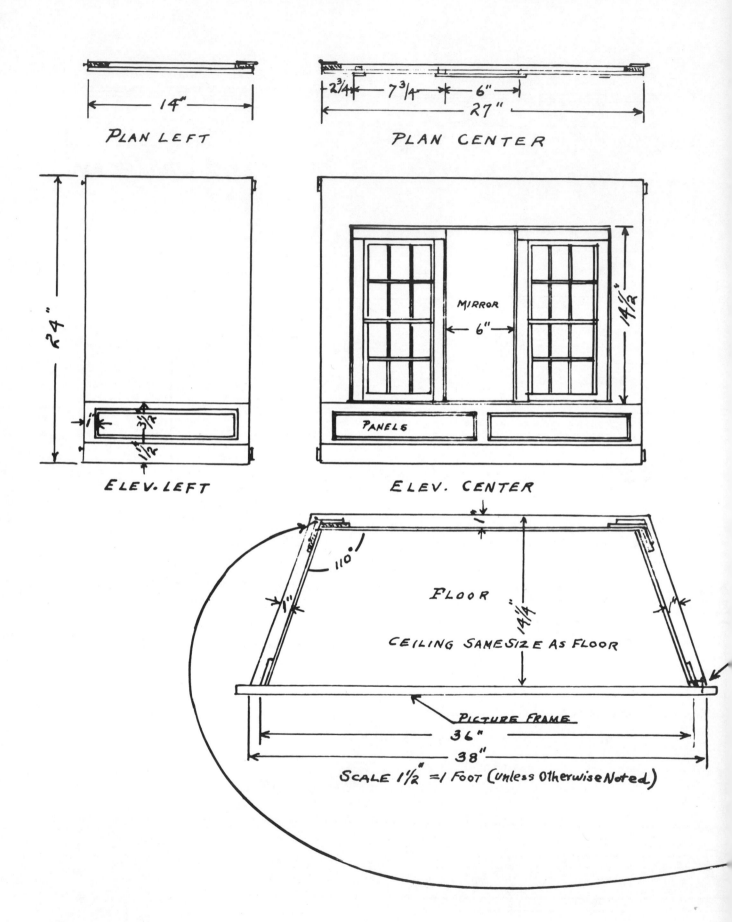

PLAN LEFT

14"

PLAN CENTER

2¾" 7¾" 6"

27"

ELEV. LEFT

24"

1" 3½" 1½"

ELEV. CENTER

MIRROR

6"

14½"

PANELS

FLOOR

CEILING SAME SIZE AS FLOOR

110°

1"

1"

1"

14¼"

PICTURE FRAME

36"

38"

SCALE 1½" = 1 FOOT (Unless Otherwise Noted)

PLATE 19.

MUSIC ROOM SETTING

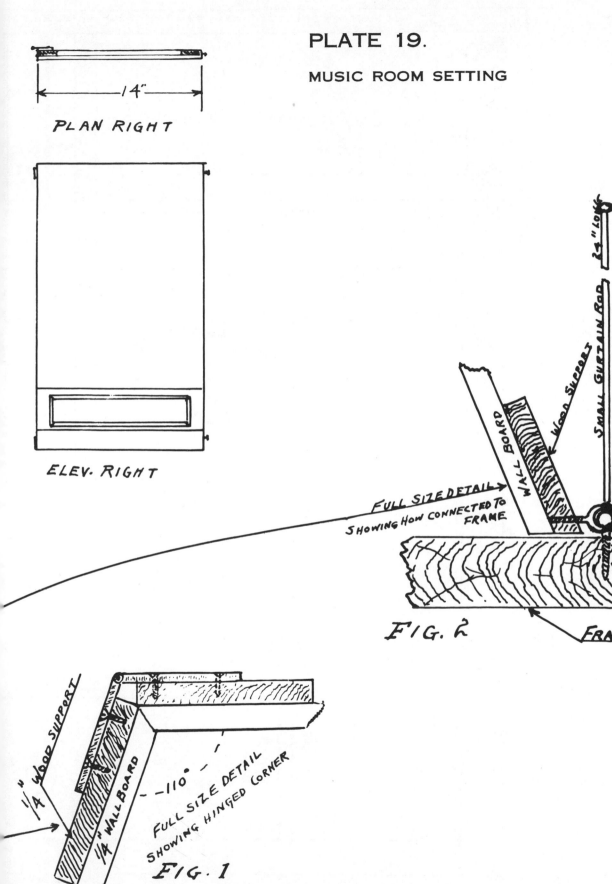

|← 14" →|

PLAN RIGHT

ELEV. RIGHT

FIG. 1

FULL SIZE DETAIL SHOWING HINGED CORNER

¼" WOOD SUPPORT

¼" WALLBOARD

110°

FIG. 2

FULL SIZE DETAIL SHOWING HOW CONNECTED TO FRAME

WALL BOARD

WOOD SUPPORT

SMALL CURTAIN ROD

2½" LONG

SCREW EYES BOTTOM AND TOP

FRAME

167

167

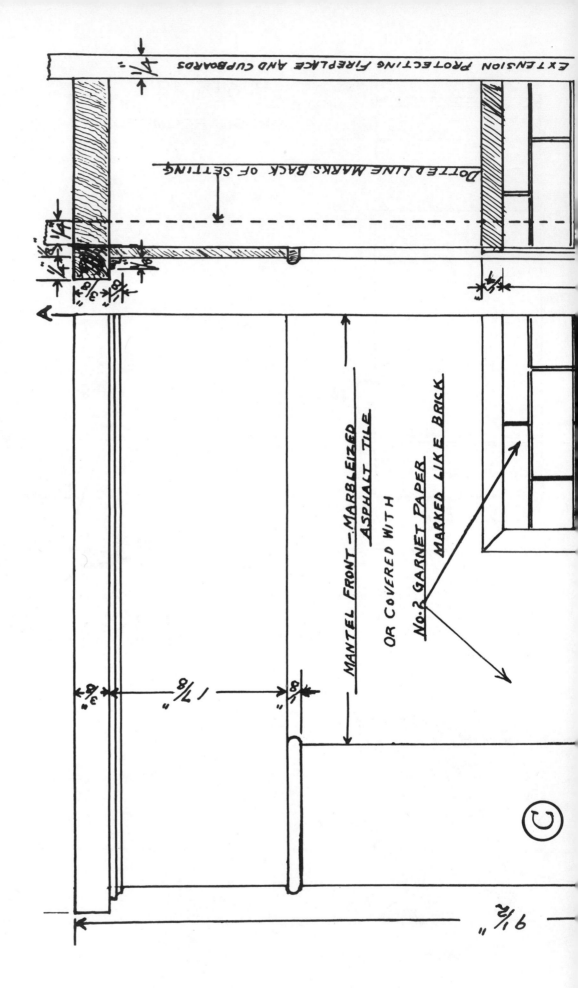

EXTENSION PROTECTING FIREPLACE AND CUPBOARDS

DOTTED LINE MARKS BACK OF SETTING

MANTEL FRONT — MARBLEIZED ASPHALT TILE OR COVERED WITH No. 2 GARNET PAPER MARKED LIKE BRICK

A

1/4"

3/8"

1/4"

1 1/2"

3/8"

1/8"

9 1/2"

C

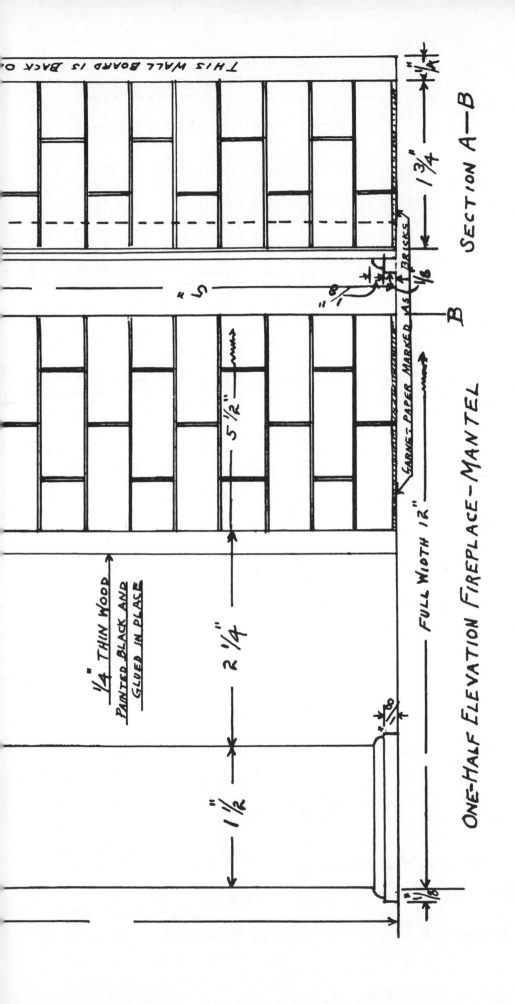

THIS WALL BOARD IS BACK O...

SECTION A—B

1 3/4"

5"

BRICKS

GARNET PAPER MARKED AS

5 1/2"

1/4" THIN WOOD
PAINTED BLACK AND
GLUED IN PLACE

2 1/4"

FULL WIDTH 12"

B

ONE-HALF ELEVATION FIREPLACE–MANTEL

1 1/2"

1/8"

FULL SIZE

PLATE 20.

DETAIL OF MANTEL AND FIREPLACE

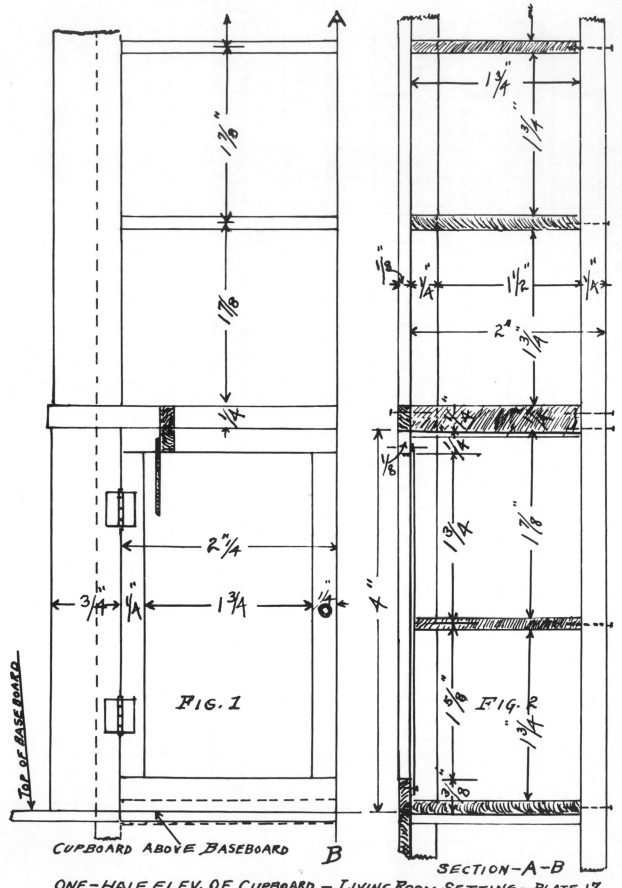

TOP OF BASEBOARD

CUPBOARD ABOVE BASEBOARD

FIG. 1

FIG. 2

SECTION—A—B

ONE—HALF ELEV. OF CUPBOARD — LIVING ROOM SETTING—PLATE 17

170

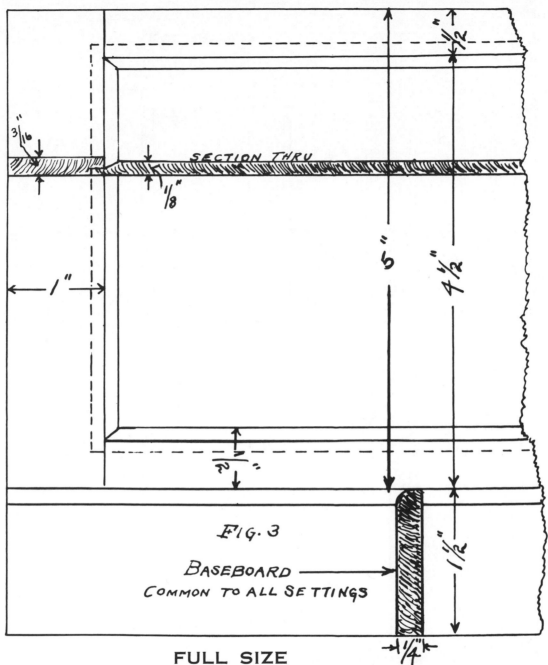

SECTION THRU

FIG. 3

BASEBOARD
COMMON TO ALL SETTINGS

FULL SIZE
DETAILS OF SHORT SECTION OF WAINSCOATING
MUSIC ROOM SETTING — PLATE 19

PLATE 21.

CUPBOARD DETAIL
WAINSCOTING SHORT SECTION DETAIL

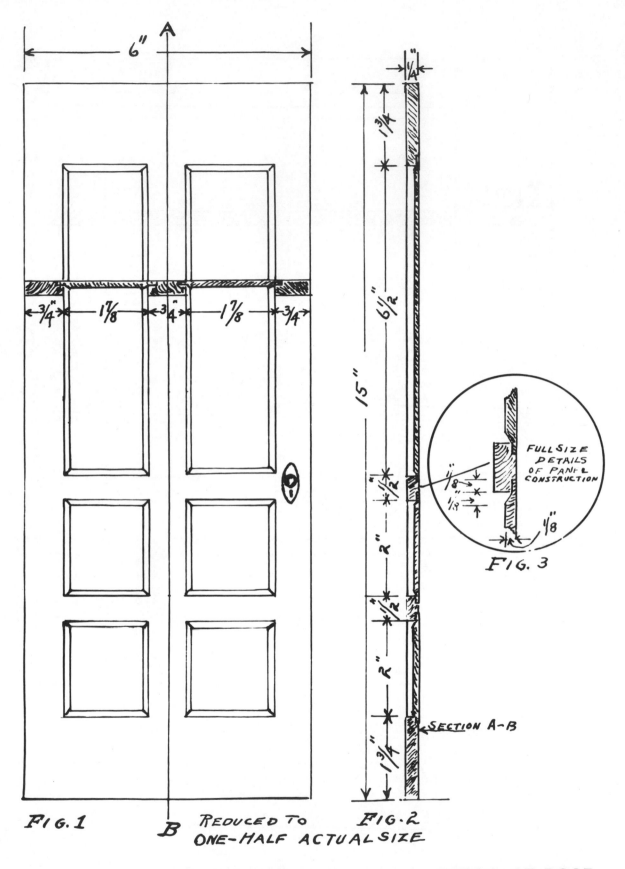

A

6"

3/4" 1⅞ 3/4" 1⅞ 3/4"

FIG. 1

B   REDUCED TO
ONE-HALF ACTUAL SIZE

¼"

1¾"

6½"

15"

½"

2"

½"

2"

1¾"

SECTION A-B

FIG. 2

FULL SIZE
DETAILS
OF PANEL
CONSTRUCTION

⅛"

⅛"

⅛"

FIG. 3

DETAIL OF DOOR

PLATE 22.

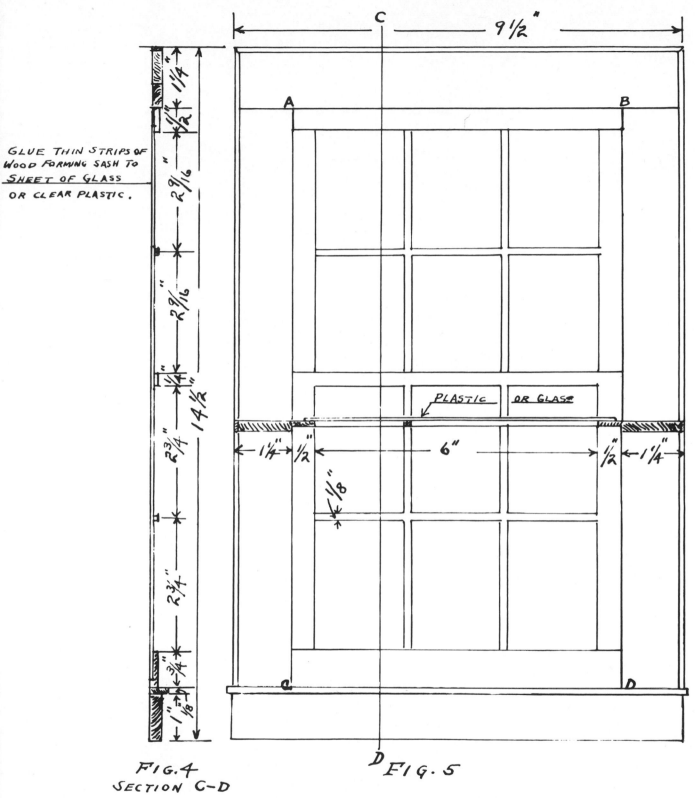

GLUE THIN STRIPS OF WOOD FORMING SASH TO SHEET OF GLASS OR CLEAR PLASTIC.

9½"

C

A   B

PLASTIC   OR GLASS

1¼" ½"   6"   ½" 1¼"

⅛"

C   D

¼"

½"

2 9/16"

2 9/16"

¼"

2¾"

14½"

2¾"

¾"

1"

⅛"

D

FIG. 4
SECTION C-D

FIG. 5

REDUCED TO ONE-HALF ACTUAL SIZE

DETAIL OF WINDOW

173

DIRECTIONS FOR MAKING
GODEY LADY DOLL
FURNITURE

ALTHOUGH handy, it is not necessary to purchase an elaborate out-lay of bench tools. All miniature furniture described herein, can be made with the commonest of equipment. Here is a list of tools, materials and finishes recommended:

TOOLS

A good, keen-bladed pocket knife; small claw hammer; cross-cut and rip saws; small wood chisels and gouges; coping saw and blades; ⅛″ and ¼″ screw drivers; combination square and level; T square; block planes; putty knife; nail set; hand drill and small bits; marking gauge; two-foot rule; compass saw; small wood rasp; three-cornered rat tail, and flat files; #00 and #1 sandpaper; oil stone; thin pointed awl; brace and bits; counter sink; small bench vice; set of carving tools; pencil compass; slip joint pliers; nippers.

LUMBER

Visit the scrap pile in your favorite lumber yard. You should be able to pick up all kinds of valuable pieces for next to nothing. Here are a few *must* articles:

Scraps of ⅛″, ¼″ and ½″ plywood in varieties of wood; white pine, red gum, birch and oak blocks 2″ x 2″, 2″ x 4″, two or more feet long; ¾″ white pine of any length; 1⁄16″, ⅛″ and ¼″ sheets of different varieties of wood usually obtainable at hobby shops; sheets of thin wood veneer; a few each of ¼″ and ½″ round sticks of wood; a paper of small pins; a box of ½″ thin brads and another of ¾″ brads; a box of small corrugated fasteners; bottle or can of liquid glue and airplane cement.

FINISHES

Assortment of oil stains — ½ pint sizes; bottle of turpentine; one pint of white shellac; one pint of clear and another of dull varnish; wood filler; plastic wood; pound can of putty; assortment of small varnish brushes.

ROSE BACK CHAIR

Not counting the upholstery and two rosettes, the chair needs but six parts. The scrolled back shown in Fig. 1, Plate 1, could be sawed out with a scroll saw from one piece of ¼″ lumber, three inches square; the seat from another piece the same size. The four legs also should offer no serious problem to make out of ¼″ stock.

The first thing, a template or pattern is made to scale of the four principal parts. Through the agency of carbon paper, the designs are transferred directly to the wood. It is a simple matter to cut out the parts, round corners, sand smooth and glue and nail in place.

Next come the ornaments. Using ⅛″ stock, the designs are scribed onto the wood, cut out and glued into place. After the glue is dry, all surplus is scraped and sanded off thoroughly, and the desired oil stain applied. This is followed by a coat of shellac and another of varnish — either gloss or dull, as preferred. Upholstery can be made from an old necktie.

CHIPPENDALE CHAIR

Draw design and make templates. See Figs. #9, #10, #11, and #12, Plate 1. After transferring designs to wood, proceed to cut each one out. To make Fig. #9, a piece of ¾″ stock is utilized, 3″ wide by 7″ long. After sawing out design with the scroll saw, the curved legs are carved out to the desired shape, then the rest of the unit is whittled down to conform to drawing. Laying this to one side, the seat is next fashioned from a piece of ⁵⁄₁₆″ stock, as per size indicated in Fig. #10. Front legs are next in order. They are carved out of ⅞″ stock with ⅛″ x ⅛″ strips glued to tops at right angles, as shown in Fig. #12. Legs are then glued and pinned in place as shown. After chair is thoroughly dry, surplus glue is scraped off and the whole sandpapered smoothly. A coat of oil stain, one of shellac and a third of varnish are next applied. When dry, the seat of chair is upholstered with a suitable pattern of small-figured brocade.

SETH-THOMAS MANTEL CLOCK

Draw a design carefully to scale. After studying, it seems that a skeleton drawing might be the best way to show the various steps in its construction. Section, Fig. K, Plate 2, is drawn along line R-R, as shown in Fig. J. First, a base is made from a solid block of wood ⅝″ thick, 1½″ wide and 2⅞″ long. The ends of this base, you will note, are notched, as per Fig. L, to receive veneer to cover rough edge. Next, a box is constructed, as per Fig. K, with a back, two sides and a top, as per dimensions given.

The front door, shown in Fig. J, is made from ⅛″ stock, cut out in one piece along lines represented by points 1 to 8. The ornaments on sides at top marked M and N are narrow wooden strips ¹⁄₁₆″ wide with square buttons of same material at top and bottom. The two small, round buttons at top on each side are cut from a round piece of wood and are ¹⁄₁₆″ thick glued in place.

At back of door a sheet of clear plastic or thin glass is glued securely. Before fastening door in place, fashion a strip of moulding ⅜″ wide by ⅜″ thick, and mitre it around clock box at top of base. Bottom of door rests on this moulding, as shown. Door is not hinged but is pinned in place for easy removal. Around top of clock box is another piece of moulding ¼″ x ¼″ which is mitred around front and two sides.

Fig. #1, made from a piece of $\frac{1}{16}''$ stock, represents the clock face support. Now, draw a design as shown on white cardboard and glue it in place on support. To secure the unit just constructed, glue strips of wood marked X and Y on both sides of clock box on the inside. Pin and glue Fig. #1 securely in place. Next make a pendulum by gluing or soldering a disc of metal to a short length of wire — the head of thumbnail tack will serve the purpose nicely. Fasten pendulum to fastener marked Z. Surmounting top of clock is the gabled bonnet. This is fashioned from $\frac{3}{16}''$ stock $2\frac{1}{2}''$ wide. The ornament in center is cut from a rounded piece of wood and glued in place, protruding about $\frac{1}{16}''$. Glue and pin this unit in place, after which when glue is sufficiently dry, scrape off surplus, and sand thoroughly. A three-coat finish — oil stain, shellac and varnish — completes the job.

VICTORIAN ROCKING CHAIR

Here is the platform rocker, Plate 3, that can still be found in some parts of America. Starting at the most important part, Fig. #1, is the correct procedure. These two parts should be cut as single units with a coping saw, using pieces of lumber about $7'' \times 7'' \times \frac{3}{16}''$ thick. A little whittling and they are the proper size. Next, the seat is cut from $\frac{5}{16}''$ stock, according to dimensions given. Pinned and glued securely to the rocker units is the seat, head-piece and back, all of which are cut from $\frac{1}{8}''$ material. The back is secured to the seat at a 100 degree angle. The rungs marked B and C are $\frac{1}{8}''$ in diameter and installed where shown. After the different units are pinned and glued together, the chair is ready to be scraped, sanded and finished. It is best to complete varnishing before attempting upholstering job. Seat, back, both front and rear and arms, should be well padded before fabric is glued and tacked into place. The arms, especially on outer side, should be well rounded. Fabric for upholstery can be any small-patterned brocade of a deep shade.

PIANO STOOL

Remember the old-fashioned piano stool, Plate 3, which as a youngster you used for a merry-go-round? That's the next project. Only three major parts to it — seat, stem, and legs. A glance at drawing is enough to show how easy it is to make and assemble. A $\frac{1}{16}''$ machine screw

178

Room setting, showing Victorian rocking chair,
piano and stool and grandfather's clock

installed not too tightly is employed to raise and lower seat. The legs, in two parts, are notched and glued together. The stem, made from ⅜″ stock, is a simple carving job. After assembly, scrape surface, sandpaper thoroughly and finish to suit taste. The seat should be padded slightly and upholstered in some black silk or faille material resembling the old horsehair.

ANDIRONS

Here is another simple carving job, Plate 3. A suitable ball for the top can either be whittled out or obtained by prowling through some feminine costume jewelry shop. The five-and-dime store should be an excellent source for stray bits of material. This ball is glued or pinned in place at top of stem, Fig. #5. One set of legs only is required for this piece. Glue or pin securely to stem. The support represented by Fig. #6 is made from a piece of ⅛″ stock and glued at top of legs in space indicated by dotted lines. Be sure to make two pairs, if both Living Room and Bed Room settings are made. After assembly is sanded, finish with a coat of flat black paint to simulate wrought iron.

SHELF OF BOOKS

From a piece of ½″ stock, Plate 3, cut out an irregular line, as shown at top. Between books make slight saw cuts, after which glue on various colored leathers marked off to simulate titles, etc., of books. Make two or three of these as needed, varying designs. These are to be displayed in bookcases shown in Living Room Setting (Plate 17).

HEPPLEWHITE CHAIR

The usual study discloses that only three major pieces are required. In Fig. #1, Plate 4, the entire back unit is a one-piece scroll saw job, cut from ⁵⁄₁₆″ stock, about 3½″ x 8″. After whittling a 93 degree slant to the back and legs, the unit is laid aside until other parts have been completed. Next, the seat is fashioned from ¼″ material, as per Fig. #3. The front legs are cut out with a taper from ¼″ at the top to ⅛″ at the bottom. The rungs, ⅛″ x ⅛″ square, are pinned and glued in place, and the rest completely assembled.

180   After scraping and sanding, the desired finish is applied — a coat

of oil stain, one of shellac and another of varnish. Now, the chair is ready for upholstering. After padding seat and edges properly, a suitable fabric is tacked and glued on, completing the project.

VICTORIAN UPHOLSTERED CHAIR

Cut out the horse-shoe shaped back with a scroll saw, using dimensions given in Fig. #5, Plate 4. Next, the part is whittled down to proper size and the edges rounded. On reverse side, pin and glue in place shown by dotted lines a back board cut from ⅛" stock. Now make the seat from ¼" material, as per dimensions given in Fig. #4. Cut the back legs tapering from ¼" at top to ⅛" at the bottom. Pin and glue parts just made to the seat. The front legs are carved out of 1" square pieces like design shown. These are glued and pinned to seat bottom, fitted against the ⅛" x ⅛" strips as shown in Fig. #7. Now glue and pin the seat with legs attached to the back unit. Fit and glue in place the side brackets, which brace the seat and back. From material, ⅛" x ¼", make the carved piece crowning back of chair and fasten in place. When dry, scrape off all surplus glue, sand thoroughly and finish with a coat of oil stain, one of shellac and another of varnish. When ready for upholstering, pad seat and back — front and rear — with cotton. Then cover with a light tan velvet, or other suitable material.

SPINET PIANO (Melodeon)

Refer to Plate 5, Fig. #2. First, four solid blocks of wood are cut and sanded down. Block marked B was 2½" wide, 1⅝" thick and 7" long. The two blocks C and C are 1⅝" x 1⅝" x 4" long. The third block marked D, 1" wide, 9⁄16" thick and 4½" long. The B and two C blocks are next mitred together at the corners as shown in Fig. #2, and joined with corrugated brads. The block D is nailed and glued solidly to block B.

The corners of blocks marked C are also rounded at the front with a 1" radius. Next, a thin sheet of veneer is glued to the rough ends of B and C. The legs are carved out of 1" stock, as per Fig. #1. Next, a bottom board is cut from ⅛" material, 4" wide by 8" long. Now, at each of the four corners as shown in Fig. 3, fasten legs to bottom board with screws, shown at F. Nail and glue bottom board to blocks B, C, and D.

Cut a top board from ⅛″ stock, round off the nose and glue to top of block B, allowing it to project over ⅛″. Next, from the same size stock, cut out and glue top boards on the C blocks, making neat joint with the board secured to block B. Still another similar board is needed to cover top of block D, showing a ¹⁄₁₆″ projection.

Forming a base for the keyboard is another block ¼″ thick, 1¹⁵⁄₁₆″ wide and 4½″ long. Now, using the design shown in Fig. 10, mark off a keyboard on a piece of ⅛″ stock. For the keys, use strips of black and white plastic glued in place. Material of this nature may be available from discarded plastic handbags. However, black and white cardboard will furnish a good substitute. When completed, glue keyboard in place where indicated. To the back and both ends of keyboard are blocks of ¼″ stock glued in place as shown in Fig. 10.

Hinged to top board of block B is a length of ⅛″ material marked G, 1½″ wide by 4⅜″ long. One-eighth inch forward from back edge of G, another piece, 1⅜″ wide by 4⅜″ long, is hinged to the former. These small hinges are readily available at your local hobby shop. The combination just formed provides a lid which when swung forward makes a covering for the keyboard.

In Fig. #8, the design for music rack is shown. It is cut from ¹⁄₁₆″ material, scroll sawed out and hinged to top board of block D. Fig. #4 depicts the pedal assembly. It is sawed from a length of ¹⁄₁₆″ stock and glued to the ⅛″ x ¼″ block shown attached to bottom board. Extending down from the same block of wood are two lengths of stiff brass wire the ends of which are secured to a block of wood fastened on the reverse side of Fig. #4. Figures #5 and #6 show how the pedals are fashioned. Cut off screw parts of two common earring bases like shown. These are easily obtainable in your local shops. Now, bend, as shown in Fig. 6; file ends of wire to sharp points and force into the bottom of block shown by dotted lines at bottom of Fig. #4.

Clean entire unit just completed thoroughly, and sand with #00 sandpaper. If a high gloss finish is desired, after applying coat of oil stain and one of shellac, give one or two coats of a good quality varnish, sanding lightly between coats. If a super gloss is desired, instead of varnish, apply a coat or two of lacquer obtainable at your hobby shop.

MID-VICTORIAN ROSE BACK SOFA (Empire)

Refer to Plate 6. The first step toward the making of this sofa is the frame shown in Figs. #1 and #3. Use ⅜″ stock, making it 3⅜″ wide by 10″ long. Up from the bottom edge of frame, nail ⅛″ x ⅛″ strips to accommodate the bottom board. Secured to the top of frame, front, back and along the sides, ⅛″ from outer edges, nail strips of ¼″ material ⁵⁄₁₆″ thick. The back strip is beveled 103 degrees to accomodate the backboard as shown in Fig. #3 and outlined in Fig. #2.

The arms are carved from blocks of soft wood about 2″ by 2″ by 3⅝″. Follow design shown by dotted lines Fig. #7. They should fit snugly against the backboard. Next, from a length of white pine, fashion a curved piece as per Fig. #6 to form the seat.

In Fig. #8, following the dotted-line design, cut out the four legs from ⅜″ stock, according to dimensions given. Now, from ⅛″ material cut out a band, following the contour of the backboard. This band ranges in size from ⅝″ wide, where it joins the ends, to ⅜″ in the center. Trace directly on wood, before cutting.

From ⅛″ stock, cut out ornamental facing shown in Fig. #4. The disks, ¾″ in diameter at each end, are cut away and the entire piece made as a unit. Next, carve out the crest, as outlined in Fig. #5., which crowns the back band. It, too, should be traced and transferred to proper stock before cutting.

Now, all is ready for assembling. Join the various parts that have been prepared, by gluing and pinning each in its proper place. When dry, scrape off surplus glue, sandpaper thoroughly and finish to suit the taste. Finally, pad lightly with cotton parts to be upholstered and cover with some heavy satin fabric in a dark shade, being sure to leave back band and arm ends bare.

OLD COLONIAL GRANDFATHER CLOCK

The base is made from a solid block of wood, as per Fig. #1, Plate 7. Four legs, ⅛″ by ⅝″ by ⅝″, are tacked to bottom. Both rough ends are covered with thin sheets of veneer and a piece of ⅛″ material ⅞″ wide is mitred, glued and pinned to front and two sides around bottom of block. Next, a length of moulding fashioned from ¼″ stock is mitred around the top of the same block.

According to dimensions afforded by Fig. #2, the middle section A-B-C-D is put together. Two sides and back are cut from ⅛″ material; bottom and top boards from ³⁄₁₆″ stock. A frontal board at the top extends down ⅞″; the board at the bottom, however, cut from the same ⅛″ material, is mitred at the ends to receive the mitred

183

ends of side pieces, as shown in Fig. #4. At the top, a ⅝″ board is nailed to the frontal piece and extends around sides. A band of moulding is nailed beneath this member across the front and sides, while a length of cove moulding serves a like purpose at the bottom. Cut a door frame, extending from frontal board F to baseboard E from a piece of ⅛″ stock, according to dimensions, as per Fig. #4. To this frame hinge slab door H.

Next construct another box cut from ⅛″ material, according to dimensions in Fig. #3. On white cardboard draw the clock face design shown in Fig. 5, and glue to a piece of ¹⁄₁₆″ material 2⅝″ wide by 3¼″ high. This is fastened inside the box to strips nailed along the side for the purpose. Now from one piece of ⅛″ material cut out the oval-topped door, 3″ wide by 3½″ high. On inside of door just made, glue a sheet of clear plastic or thin glass. Pin door securely to frame. A length of ³⁄₁₆″ moulding is next fastened in place across front and two sides.

Bonnet, shown in Fig. #6 consists of a gabled piece of ¼″ material, 3¼″ long by 1″ wide at peak of gable. To the front of this piece is tacked a ⁵⁄₁₆″ moulding projecting ⅛″ over each edge. The pendulum consists of a metal disk about ⅝″ in diameter soldered to a stiff piece of brass wire, which is secured to top board of Fig. #4.

After all units are made and assembled, scrape and sandpaper thoroughly. Then, apply a coat of oil stain of the desired shade followed with a coat of shellac and a finish coat of varnish.

COLONIAL SPINNING WHEEL

Here's a piece of furniture, Plate 8, that calls for each piece being fashioned separately before assembling is attempted. By studying drawing carefully, it is easy to see how best to proceed. Bench block, shown in Fig. #3, should be made first. It is cut from ⁵⁄₁₆″ material. First consider the under side of bench block. Now, mark off and drill ⅛″ holes according to slant indicated. There are but three holes to be bored, two for the back legs, marked E in Fig. #1, and only one for the front leg, marked D.

Next, repeat the performance on the top side of bench block. You will note, there are five holes to be drilled. Now carve the legs and standards from oak or other sturdy material. When finished, lay aside awaiting final assembly.

With coping saw, from $\frac{1}{16}''$ material, cut out driving wheel, according to diagram in Fig. #1. Make two identical parts. Bevel inside edges of both with rasp. Take care that they fit perfectly, forming a grooved track for the drive belt. Now glue the two parts together, holding them firmly together with clamps. Next, fashion spindle pulley from a piece of $\frac{1}{4}''$ stock, cutting groove to accomodate the belt.

By consulting plan, Fig. #2, which affords a view looking down to bench block, it is easier to understand how spindle marked F is constructed. A loose wire shaft runs through holes drilled in standards B-B. First, the shaft is run through hole in the left standard. It is then forced through pulley making a tight fit. A small wooden washer $\frac{1}{4}''$ in diameter is slipped over the end of shaft against the pulley. Another washer the same size is also slipped over the end of shaft tightly to form the right side of the spindle. When assembled, the ends of shaft wire are bent so they cannot slip out of their bearings.

Next, from a length of small stiff wire, make a front shaft bent to the shape shown in Fig. #2. Slip end of shaft through hole in left side support A. Shaft should fit loosely. Now, force a wooden washer like shown in diagram tightly in place just left of center between supports. The driving wheel is next forced on shaft and against the first washer, and finally force on the second washer to a position against second standard and bend wires to keep in place.

In Fig. #5, the treadle is shown. It extends from rear leg, marked E, to which it is attached with a loose pin, to the treadle upright in Fig. #1. Everything is now ready to assemble. Glue legs in place and install standards with driving wheel and spindle, as previously instructed. Next, attach treadle upright to drive shaft and finish up by attaching treadle to rear leg E and then to treadle upright. It may take some adjusting, before spinning wheel will function, but by using perseverance, it should be made to operate satisfactorily.

EARLY AMERICAN WING-BACK CHAIR

Plate 9 shows the design of a chair that should be easy to construct. There are but four major parts. According to dimensions and contours shown in Fig. #1, cut out with coping saw the side, arm and back legs, in one piece, from $\frac{1}{4}''$ stock, being careful to observe the 97 degree angle between seat and back. Make two of these identical.

In Fig. #2 and Fig. #3 the seat and back are shown. Both are cut from ¼″ material of sizes and shapes indicated. Next, carve out the two front legs as depicted in Fig. #4. Now, pin and glue seat and back securely in place. Screw on front legs in position, as shown in Fig. #10.

After scraping and sanding thoroughly, chair is ready for varnishing. This should not be a big job, as the four legs are all the parts requiring such treatment. After varnish is dry, the chair is ready for upholstering. Pad seat, arms, back and wings with cotton, rolling arms on outer sides. It is well to use a small wooden cylinder, about the size of a lead pencil, well padded with cotton and secured in place at top of arms on the outside, before covering with fabric. After this has been completed, cover reverse side of back with the same material.

COLONIAL HIGH-BACK WALL STAND

This piece of furniture consists of four major parts. First, consult Plate 9. The first step is to cut from ¼″ material the top and back according to dimensions given in Figs. #5 and #8. Next, carve out the pedestal from one-inch stock. As indicated in Fig. #6, the upper part, just beneath the square board, ⅛″ by 1¼″ by 1¼″, is octagonal in shape — one inch at top tapering down to ⅝″ at bottom. The ½″ thick base is cut round, as per diagram Fig. #9.

Now, cut out from ¼″ material and notch together the two legs as per diagram in Fig. #7. It should be noted that one is notched at the top and the other at the bottom, so they will fit together flush at the top. Glue and pin legs together and everything is ready to assemble. In like manner, fasten back securely along rear edge of stand top. Nail and glue the ⅛″ by 1¼″ by 1¼″ square piece to top of pedestal. Now, screw stand top to pedestal, counter-sinking screw and filling in depression with plastic wood. Next, secure leg assembly to bottom of pedestal.

After a thorough scraping and sanding finish with a coat of oil stain followed by one of clear shellac and another of varnish.

FRENCH EMPIRE CRYSTAL CHANDELIER

In one of the great Park mansions, named "Strawberry", hangs an ancient crystal chandelier from which this miniature replica was copied, Plate 10. This is a number that will tax the ingenuity but, by following carefully the various steps, it should not be found too difficult to manage.

Starting with Fig. #1 and progressing, the parts should be made, and laid aside for final assembly. First, using a piece of one-inch material, carve out top piece as per dimensions given. Now, cut a circular piece of plastic or reasonably stiff leather, represented by A, ¾″ in diameter. In this disk, puncture twenty-four holes around the margin about ¹⁄₁₆″ from edge. Next, cut another disk of same material, B, 3¼″ in diameter, and puncture twenty-four tiny holes in it to compare with those cut in disk, A.

Fig. #4, represents a disk of ¼″ wooden material, which supports the central part of chandelier. Now, cut a third disk, C, from plastic or leather, using a 3⅞″ diameter. Along the margin, puncture forty-one small holes. Still another disk of the same material is required, marked D, one inch in diameter. Forty-one small holes should be punctured along its margin.

Fig. #7 represents a wood carving from a piece of ⅜″ material with top diameter ⅞″ and a bottom one of ⅝″. This part should be of oak or other kind of sturdy wood not apt to split. A ⅛″ depression is hollowed out of the under side, as shown. It is to accommodate the turned end of ¹⁄₁₆″ wire.

In Fig. #8, a length of brass wire about ¹⁄₁₆″ in diameter is shown. It has a hook at top to be used in hanging finished chandelier to ceiling of Living Room Setting, Plate 17.

Around central disk, Fig. #4, is fastened a band of bright ornamental metal about one-half inch wide. Fig. #9 depicts the kind of edging used. It is a dime-store barette, and should not be difficult to duplicate. If not one exactly like the sample, others may be obtainable as substitute. The one shown is about ½″ wide and 2¼″ long. About six of such would be required to encircle the disk. This ornamental band should be sufficiently pliable to bend around the circular disk without breaking. If nothing of the nature described is obtainable, a band of filigreed metal, or even a plain strip of brass would do. A little perserverance in the search should be used.

Now, it is time to start stringing beads. Obtain a spool of strong white thread — number 40 should do. Visit your five-and-dime store again and obtain two vials of crystal beads — one vial of short ones, about ¹⁄₁₆″ in diameter and a like amount of longer ones, about ¼″ long, as shown in Fig. #12. String beads, first a long bead and then a short one, making strands of sufficient length to festoon gracefully between anchorages. Each strand in top section, of which there are twenty-four, should measure approximately 3⅝"; the ones in the lower section, forty-one in number, should measure about 2¾" long. Lengths quoted are not absolute, as beads vary in sizes somewhat and adjustments have to be made to suit the individual case. Now, fasten top strands to disk A and B and lay aside for final assembly. Next, adopt same procedure on disks C and D.

Fig. #11, shows how the candelabra is prepared. To fashion the individual candle holders, utilize dime-store earring bases, as shown in Fig. #10. Nip off the cupped disk and, with a sharp awl puncture a hole in it large enough to receive a small length of brass wire, bent as shown in Fig. #11 and pointed on the reverse end. Solder or glue the formed wire holder to disk. Make ten of this unit.

Everything should now be ready for final assembly. Drill holes in Figs. #1, #4 and #6 small enough to accommodate wire shaft shown in Fig. #8. This must be a tight fit. Now, thrust wire through hole in Fig. #1 and down through hole in plastic disks A and B, thence through center disk, Fig. #4, on through plastic disks C and D, and finally through Fig. #7. Turn end of wire L shape and fit in hollowed out crevice prepared for the purpose in the bottom of Fig. #7. Now, adjust center disk to position as shown in Fig. #12. A little manipulating here and there should place everything in its proper position. A drop of liquid solder dropped on each junction of brass wire, Fig. #8, with wooden members, will further guarantee against slipping.

Next, force sharp ends of candle holders into central wooden disk, as shown. For candles, use short lengths of the very small ones used on birthday cakes. A drop of melted wax will suffice to hold them in place.

Finally, apply one or two coats of bronze or gold paint to all exposed wooden surfaces.

HARP (French Empire)

On Plate 11 is depicted another of the antique treasures of "Strawberry Mansion". There are but five parts. A study of the design shows how easy it should be to assemble, once all parts have been constructed. Starting at the base, cut out member represented by Fig. #6 from a solid block of ⅞" material, using dimensions and contour indicated. Where shown, cut mortices in face of block — see Figs. #4 and #6 — giving each the proper degree of slant. Next, cut out soundboard, according to dimensions indicated in Fig. #3. Cut mortices at top and tenon at bottom.

The neck piece is fashioned from ½" thick material of size and shape shown in Fig. #2 with tenons at each end. Along top margin, make and put into place twenty wrest pins, which are carved from ⅛" stock with rounded heads. Force medium loosely in small holes previously drilled.

The pillar, as per Fig. #1 is carved from one-inch material. Transfer design to wood block that is to be carved, to afford facility to the operation. Cut out mortice at top to accommodate neck tenon and a tenon at bottom to fit into mortice in base. The top of pillar at A-B offers an excellent spot for working out a design. If desirable, mix a small quantity of plaster of Paris with water to which is added about 10% by volume of common wheat flour. The flour keeps plaster from drying too hard. When of a consistency about like putty, apply a coating to the wood, which has been previously coated with liquid glue. When partly dry, with a knife or other tool cut out the desired design.

When all members are cut and fitted properly, glue and pin the various parts together. Now cut a groove in sound board sufficient to accommodate a piece of leather, wood or plastic, which should be glued in place and act as an anchor for thin brass wires. On base, between pedestal and sound board, glue another piece of like material for the same purpose. Now, string very fine brass or copper wire between these anchorages and the wrest pins in the neck of instrument. Tighten wires as needed by twisting pins.

When completely assembled, cleaned and scraped and sanded, finish with two coats of gold or bronze gilt paint.

COLONIAL CRADLE

A study of Plate 12 will prove to any determined whittler how easy it should be to make this cradle. It comprises only a half-dozen major parts. The first thing is making the sides. There are two of them just alike. Using ⅛" material, construct a frame as per Fig. #1. On reverse side, glue and pin strip of ¹⁄₁₆" stock, as shown by dotted lines. Next, make a similar frame for the front end, according to dimensions given in Fig. #2. In a similar manner, construct the other end of the same width but only 2¼″ high.

Now, from ¼″ square material, cut out a pair of front, and a like number of back legs, both sets having turned tops, as shown, and notched bottoms for securing rockers.

The rockers, shown in Fig. #3 should be fashioned from ⅛″ material of size and contour indicated. Next, cut out two side brackets, as per Fig. #5, using ⅛″ stock. Secure them, one on either side of cradle, as and where indicated.

When all component members are prepared, start assembling. Pin and glue sides and ends to legs in manner outlined. Next, secure rockers to bottom of legs. After all parts are placed properly and thoroughly dry, scrape off surplus glue, sandpaper thoroughly and complete job by applying a coat of oil stain, one of shellac and another of clear varnish.

EARLY AMERICAN WASHSTAND

First, make the box-like unit as per Fig. #1, Plate 13, from ⅛″ material; glue and pin securely together. The front end of this member consists of a frame of a size to accommodate the drawer, shown in Figs. #2 and #4. The front piece of drawer is grooved and beveled off to fit front of frame. A study of Fig. #4 will enable one to understand how the member is put together. In rear of drawer is a strip of ⅛″ material nailed in place to serve as a stop. At top is another strip of the same material nailed across depth of stand on each side to act as a glide. When cutting out drawer, be sure a small clearance of approximately ¹⁄₁₆″ is allowed to insure freedom of action.

The four legs are identical, being cut from ⅜″ stock, tapered down from ⅜″ at the top to ¼″ at bottom. Nail and glue them securely to under side of box-like unit. Across back of stand is the splash board, cut from ⅛″ material and nailed along rear edge of stand top. It is rounded along top edge. The side pieces are cut from same size stock, according to dimension and contour shown in Fig. #3. Near the bottom of legs, Fig. #2, is shown a shelf cut from ⅛″ material, glued and pinned to the four legs. A support of the same thickness and ³⁄₁₆″ wide is secured to shelf and legs where shown.

When completely assembled and dry, scrape and sand thoroughly, and finish with oil stain, shellac and varnish in order named.

EARLY AMERICAN HIGHBOY

Plate 14 depicts a replica of a Highboy. In reality this piece of antiquity consists of a double chest of drawers mounted on legs. The one from which this miniature descended stood a trifle over five feet high.

Again, here is a piece that requires but three major parts. Fig. #1, the upper chest of drawers, is constructed, as per diagram, in the upper portion of Fig. #3. First, a box is made, using ⅛″ material on the two sides, back and bottom. The top is formed by another piece of ⅛″ stock with rounded edges, front and side, projecting over ¼″ with a strip of ⅛″ moulding along the under side.

The front of this unit consists of a frame, like the one shown in Fig. #1 and Section G-G, Fig. #3. Care should be exercised in installing cross sections according to detailed dimensions given.

All drawers are made very much alike. By constructing one, the procedure governing the next is comparatively easy. Drawer A is typical. The only difference is in size. Some are larger, others smaller, but all are made similarly.

Drawer A in Fig. #3 is made to fit opening indicated, 1⅛″ high by 4¾″ wide. Make, from ⅛″ material, a simple box just a trifle smaller than dimensions given, to insure ease of movement. Guides are shown at top and bottom of each drawer. They are nailed securely in place, to keep unit in place when opening and closing. The front member is cut from a piece of the same ⅛″ stock about ⅛″ wider than vertical dimension indicated. This part is cut out as shown in A and bevelled along each outside edge, before being pinned and glued to front of drawer. In like manner the others are made, using dimensions given for each individual one.

The bottom section of Highboy should be made as an irregular box, outlined by points A-B-C-D-E-F, following dotted lines in Fig. #2. It is 5½″ long at top, 2″ high at sides and 2⅜″ wide at ends. The bottom part of box is the irregular part, being 1¹¹⁄₁₆″ wide from each side across the bottom, thence upward ¹⁵⁄₁₆″ from that point, and then at right angles to meet other side of box.

The front of this unit should be sawed from one piece of ⅛″ material, 5½″ by 2⅛″ wide. Then, following the contour indicated by C-D the design shown at bottom of front should be transferred directly to piece of material and cut out with scroll saw. After drawer openings have been cut away, according to dimensions given in Fig. #2, the front should be nailed and glued to front part of box.

Next, carve out legs as per contour indicated in Fig. #5. Fit to all four corners, according to diagram in Fig. #4, screwing securely in place. When work is dry enough, scrape off any surplus glue, sandpaper thoroughly and finish with a coat of oil stain, a second of shellac, and a third one of varnish.

EARLY AMERICAN SECRETARY

Like so many pieces of colonial furniture this early American secretary, Plate 15, is also made in sections. In this particular instance, there are three of them — upper, middle and lower, each of which is constructed independently of the other.

First, the upper portion is made box-like, using ¼″ material for sides, back, top, and bottom. Nail together securely. Next in order is the installation of shelves which are made from ⅛″ stock in positions shown, using dimensions indicated. Now, cutting along points ABCD, construct two doors, from ⅛″ stock, each in one piece, using scroll saw to make openings representing window panes. On reverse sides of doors, glue a strip of clear plastic to simulate glass. To further secure same, bind along edges with scotch tape. Doors as indicated are hinged to frame. Small hinges of this nature may be obtained at your local hobby shop.

The middle section is also constructed in box form, using ¼″ material for back and sides and ⅛″ stock for top and bottom. The bottom however, instead of being same width as the top of this unit, is 3⅜″ long. This section also, instead of being 5½″ wide like the upper one, is 6″ in extent. It is 1¼″ high, with a bottom that forms the top of the lower section.

The front of this unit is made according to Fig. #2. At top is a strip ⅛″ thick by ¼″ wide which extends from sides to the ornamental member in center, shown in Fig. #5. This ornamental member is 1⅛″ high and 1¼″ wide with carved sunburst above and a simulated drawer below.

The lower section consists of a box-like structure. As before mentioned, the top of this member of ⅛″ material is also the bottom board of the middle section. The sides, back and bottom are constructed from ¼″ stock nailed securely together. In the front, the position of each division member should be carefully observed, as they are so located in order to make dividers for the three drawers.

The method used in constructing the drawers has been fully covered by descriptive matter concerning similar members in making Highboy, Plate 14.

Immediately below top of this section is shown a space ¼″ wide reserved for writing-top support. This member is designed to slide back to a hidden position marked "stop", when not in use holding up the hinged portion M.

Hinged to the stationary top, L, is a hinged portion of writing table, identified as M. This member is cut from ⅛″ stock and is 1½″ wide by a trifle less than 5″ long. When not in use, fold it up as indicated by dotted line in Fig. #2.

On either side of top L is a triangular member, marked K, as shown in Fig. #1. This part is cut from ⅜″ stock and is glued and pinned securely to stationary writing top L.

Crowning top of upper section is the bonnet. This member is cut from ³⁄₁₆″ material of size and contour indicated in Fig. #3. Transfer design direct to wood, before cutting out. After rounding edges, and gluing narrow ¹⁄₁₆″ strip on top, which extends over edges as shown, secure member firmly to position.

The four legs are carved from ¾″ stock. Adhere to dimensions and contour shown in Fig. #1. Screw solidly to bottom section, using leg assembly method as per Fig. #4. The ornamental bracket-like members, adjoining legs at bottom of the section are cut out of ¹⁄₁₆″ material, and secured in place as indicated. Carve from ¼″ stock the nobbed pulls and use on drawers, doors, etc.

After all parts are assembled and glue has dried thoroughly, scrape off surplus, sand smoothly and finish with a coat of oil stain, followed by one of shellac and another of varnish.

FOUR POSTER CANOPY BED
(American about 1800)

Here on Plate 16 is depicted a replica of a very early American canopy bed — cord springs and all. It should not be difficult to reproduce.

First, whittle out, using ⅜″ material, the four identical legs, according to dimensions and contour outlined in Fig. #2. Cut mortices, where shown. Next from a sheet of ⅛″ stock cut out the backboard. Transfer the design at top and along sides direct to wood and cut out with scroll saw. Leave tenons, where indicated on end of backboard and the four rails. The latter are cut from ⅛″ material. On the top edges of them, cut out and secure knobs about ½″ apart. These are to anchor the cord spring, which interlaces across bed from side to side and from end to end.

Cut canopy framework from ⅛″ material, and glue and pin same to outside of four posts at the top. Now, stretch the canopy covering tightly over the entire top of bed, and make and hang a narrow valance or ruffle covering side pieces of canopy framework.

When all parts are completely assembled and glue is dry, **scrape** off surplus, sandpaper smoothly and apply a coat of oil stain followed by a coat each of shellac and varnish.

OLD COLONIAL LIVING ROOM SETTING

First, starting with the central portion, cut a piece of wall board (not plaster board) 3′-6¾″ wide by 1′-10″ high. To prevent warping, reinforce all along outer edges, with strips of wood ½″ thick by 2″ wide. Next, at the center of member, cut away wallboard to accommodate fireplace and two cupboards. To be more specific, starting from the center, cut out a space from the backboard of setting, measuring 5½″ wide by 5″ high. Now with a piece of the same wallboard, 6″ wide by 5½″ high, glue on a piece of garnet red paper the same size, marked off like bricks. To this attach two side wings, 1¾″ wide by 5½″ high, with garnet paper glued on, marked to simulate bricks, using gummed tape for the purpose. Both of side pieces should be butted against the back piece and secured firmly. The whole unit should then be attached to wallboard back. The bottom piece, consisting of a piece of garnet paper scored to look like brick should be fitted at the bottom where shown.

Next cut out a portion of the back of setting for the cupboards. Instead of using wallboard, employ pieces of ¼″ stock, 1″ wide by 18″ high for sides and the same stock 6″ wide for backs. For constructing both fireplace and cupboards shown in Living Room Setting, see full size details on Plates 20 and 21.

Along bottom edge of setting, using ¼″ material, install baseboard 1½″ wide with rounded nose as shown in plate 21, Fig. #3. Left and right wing sections are both made in a similar manner utilizing ¼″ wallboard reinforced at edges.

In left wing is a door, which is built flat against and glued to the

An old Colonial living room setting

wall. See details for making same, reduced to one-half size as shown on Plate 22. The same size and type of baseboard along bottom edges of all settings are identical.

In the right wing is a window. This calls for wallboard back being cut away and removed only in that portion occupied by the window sash and needs no boxed out structure behind it. For details, see Plate 22.

The floor consisting of a piece of ¼″ plywood, is four feet and four inches wide at front edge, three feet, seven and one-half inches at the back and one foot ten inches from center to center of front and back lines. At center of mantel, in line with outside confines of breast, glue on the floor a piece of red garnet paper marked off to simulate large brick for a hearthstone. The balance of floor is covered all over with a carpet of dark red plush or velvet.

For method of constructing floor support, refer to diagram marked "A", Plate 18. This support is constructed from ¾″ by 3″ material an inch or so smaller than the floor itself. The floor is nailed securely to this support or platform, flush with the front edge.

A frame, constructed from ¾″ by 4″ material, two inches or more wider than the setting and coated with gold paint, completes the front of setting. If available, an antique gold frame is ideal for the purpose mentioned.

At top and bottom of both wings, central unit and frame, screw eyes are installed, which when properly aligned permit small metal rods to be slipped into place, tying all units and frame securely together. For correct method of procedure, see full size details in Fig. #2, Plate 19.

The ceiling consists of a piece of plywood or wallboard well fortified against warping. In the center of the ceiling is a screw eye designed to hold up chandelier. Walls and ceiling should be covered with suitable paper, in a small pattern.

All woodwork when completed should receive two coats of flat gray paint.

COLONIAL BEDROOM SETTING

Like the Living Room Setting, this too has three main parts — center and right and left wings. The dimensions and baseboard also are the same, but there the similarity ends. In the central panel, five inches apart from casing to casing, are the two identical windows. These call for wallboard to be cut away along the sash lines. Although there is a deviation in size of window panes, the general principle of construction is the same. For details, reduced one half, see Fig. #5, Plate 22.

In the left wing is a fireplace, flanked on each side by a cupboard. This member is made in a manner similar to the one detailed in Plate 20. Instead of a square fireplace mouth, it has a rounded top and instead of projecting behind the backboard of setting, it extends into the room. The 1¼″ mantel top, with ¼″ projection, extends entirely across both mantel and cupboards. The dimensions governing the other parts of this number are virtually the same as the one described in Living Room Setting, Plate 17. The fireplace opening is enclosed on each side and on the bottom in a box-like confine, marked off like brick. The space on back wall in rear of mouth and the floor of opening, receives a like treatment.

The floor support is virtually the same as that described in **Plate 17**, the reverse side of which is shown in diagram A. A single piece of plywood or rigid wallboard, well reinforced, forms the ceiling. This should be painted a light color. All other wall space in setting is covered with wallpaper of a small stripe design. Woodwork should be coated with two coats of flat, off-white paint.

MUSIC ROOM SETTING

This setting is smaller than the other two, Plate 19. The central unit is 27″ wide by 24″ high and the two wings identical, 14″ wide by 24″ high. All three panels have the same ½″ by 2″ reinforcing strips along all edges in the back. A panelled wainscoating above the baseboard is common to all three units. For full sized details see Plate 21, Fig. #3.

The middle unit has twin windows six inches apart. Occupying the space between is a mirror which extends from top of wainscoating to upper surface of window casing. These windows similar to the one described and shown in detail, Plate 22, Fig. #5. Like the others, these windows call for the wallboard to be cut away along sash lines.

The method of joining the three wall units together varies from that prescribed for the other two settings. The wings are hinged onto the center unit as per full size details in Fig. #1. They are attached to the frame, however, with the screw eye and metal rod method, as outlined in Fig. #2.

The walls should receive treatment similar to that recommended for those of Plates 17 and 18.

The floor support member is constructed after the same general method as prescribed for that of the Bed Room Setting, Plate 18, with sizes reduced. A layer of blue velvet or dark red should cover the floor while a light shade of wallpaper should be used on the walls. The ceiling, consisting of a sheet of plywood should be painted a light neutral color. The woodwork can be painted with some grayed neutral shade.

FULL SIZE DETAILS OF MANTEL

Plate 20 shows a full sized detail of the living room mantel. This member is built flat against the back of setting. Only fire chamber projects behind the line as shown in section A-B and described fully in comments governing treatment for Plate 17.

The mantel top, ⅜″ thick by 12½″ wide, projects out from back wall ⅜″. The fascia board, cut from ⅛″ stock is 1⅞″ wide by 12″ long and extends across the mantel breast. It is crowned by a strip of ⅛″ moulding. Flanking sides of mantel front are two columns, marked C. They are crowned, just beneath the fascia board, with a ⅛″ strip, ¼″ wide, with rounded edges and ends. Columns are based on ⅛″ block, 1¾″ long by ⁵⁄₁₆″ wide, with ⅛″ moulding above block, turned around base of column.

If mantel breast is covered with a sheet of marbleized tile, a revision of dimensions must be made. The mantel top will be ½″ wide with the same projection as outlined above, but the fascia board must be ¼″ thick and grooved out along bottom edge to receive the tile. The same goes for the columns, the moulding crowning them and the block base. Each must have ⅛″ added to thickness or width as the case may be. If however, red garnet paper marked off as brick is used, the dimensions previously given are to be used.

Outlining fireplace opening is a strip of material cut from ¹⁄₁₆″ stock, ¼″ wide, painted flat black and glued securely around the opening. Woodwork is coated with a color in keeping with that used on rest of room.

Detail of a period living room setting

199

DETAILS OF CUPBOARDS

On Plate 21 is shown full size details of cupboards in Living Room Setting, Plate 17. These cupboards are 18″ high from floor line. The cupboard portion rests on the top of baseboard and juts back of the wallboard backing as was described in comments covering Plate 17.

Each of the cupboards has a pair of doors only one of which is shown in the detail, and two shelves spaced as indicated. Each door is 4″ high and is made by gluing a strip of veneer or ¹⁄₁₆″ material to the reverse side, according to dimensions as per Fig. #1.

The upper portion of unit consists of five shelves divided equally in the available space. Each cupboard in common with the openings in all settings is bordered with casings of ⅛″ stock, three quarters of an inch wide.

DETAILS OF WAINSCOATING

On Plate 21 is also shown full size details of a typical portion of the panelled wainscoat which can be observed just above baseboard in the Music Room Setting, Plate 19. The bottom of this member rests on the top of baseboard, as indicated. A framework identical in outline is prepared for each section of it. It is constructed of top and bottom rails joined to the end or middle rails, as the case may be. The section through the strip of wainscoat shows the method used in membering the panel to the rails. All junctions are performed in the same manner. Frame is morticed all around to receive tenons, which are cut on ends and sides of panel parts. When fitted together, they are pinned and glued securely in place and cemented to the back of setting sections. When completed, finish with whatever color is desirable.

DETAILS OF DOOR

On Plate 22 is the detail of the door used in Living Room Setting, Plate 17. It has been reduced to one-half of exact size. Exact measurements to use in constructing this door, however, have been indicated.

Refer to Fig. #1, showing the finished door, and to Fig. #2, outlining a section through the center of the door, to observe the method used in its construction. First a slab is cut from ¼″ material,

Detail of bedroom setting

The other end of bedroom setting, showing the Colonial bed

6″ wide by 15″ long. Next, after carefully outlining dimensions directly on the slab, with coping saw, cut out the panels one by one. All along margins of panel openings, on reverse side of door, using method outlined in Fig. #3, mortice for the panel tenons. Now cut the panels from ⅛″ material. Bevel as shown and make tenons. As each one is fitted properly, glue into place. When door is finished, carve out a handle knob and escutcheon and glue them to door at proper place.

DETAILS OF TYPICAL WINDOW

Windows for all settings are made from the same general pattern as outlined in Fig. #5, Plate 22. The only material difference is width and variance in length.

Cut from back wall of setting a space governed by the size of the sash part of each drawing. After bordering opening with casing, window stool and apron, take a sheet of clear, stiff plastic or thin window glass, one-half inch larger all around than the opening it is to cover. Next outline on the sheet of glass or plastic the dimensions of sash and window pane bars. Now, cut strips of ¹⁄₁₆″ stock of the proper dimensions to make the sash sides and bars and glue them in place directly to glass or plastic. After these members are perfectly dry, glue the completed part to the back of setting, being certain that sash exactly fits the opening. To make more secure, bind along the edges of glass or plastic on reverse side of setting with strips of gummed tape. When this unit is finished and secured in place, apply two or more coats of paint in keeping with colors used in rest of setting.

BED TICK AND BOLSTER

Cut out two strips of muslin 14½″ long by 10½″ wide, and another of the same material 2½″ wide by 45″ long. Now sew the two larger strips to the narrow one, using the latter for a divider. Be certain, however, to leave a small vent at one side for stuffing purposes. Next, fill the casing so made with cotton or kapok, with well-rounded top to simulate an old-fashioned bed tick. The bolster is made by sewing together a strip of the same material and stuffing with cotton or kapok. The dimension of this member should be approximately 8″ long by 7″ around.

DUST RUFFLES

Using white muslin edged along bottom and sides with heavy lace, make dust ruffles approximately 2½" wide, one for each side of bed and another for the foot. These should be sewed to the tick, so that they extend almost to the floor.

BED SPREAD

This item can either be crocheted from cotton yarn by one reasonably expert with the hooked needle, or fashioned from white or cream-colored brocade or net, with a small pattern of some sort interwoven. The spread when finished should be long enough to fold over bolster, and sufficiently wide to meet dust ruffles at top edges.

INDEX

A

Accessories, *See patterns*
Alexander Doll Co., 46
Alice, 27, 28, 35, 45
Andirons, 180
Angel doll, 46
Antoinette, Marie, 1
Apron — Mammy doll, 117
Architecture, 17
Arizona, 48
Art Institute, 27
Art museum, 41
Artist — fashion, 9, 10
Autobiography, Sarah Hale, Introduction
Awakening, intellectual, 2, 4
Awl, *See tools*

B

Baby, 21
Bassinet, 46
Bastard of fashion, 11
Beads, *See patterns*
Bed, four-poster, 193
Bedroom, 196, 197
Bedspread, 203
Bed tick — Bolster, 202
Bench vice, *See tools*
Bertha, *See patterns*
Bevel, *See tools*
Bible of the parlor, 2
Birch, *See lumber*
Blackwell, Elizabeth, 8
Block plane, *See tools*
Body, doll's, 22, 52

Books, shelf, 180
Boots, 58
Boston, 3
Brace, *See tools*
Brads, *See tools*
Braid, *See patterns*
Bricks, fireplace, 194
Bride doll, 36
Broadcloth, *See patterns*
Bryant, 9
Buckram, *See patterns*
Bustle, *See patterns*
Buttons, *See patterns*

C

Calicoe, 117
Can can dancer, 22
Candelabra, 188
Canopy, 194
Carpet, *See rooms*
Carving, *See furniture*
Casting, doll's head, 51
Ceiling, *See rooms*
Chair — Instructions:
    Chippendale, 177
    Heppelwhite, 180
    Rose back, 176
    Victorian rocker, 178
    Victorian upholstered, 181
    Wingback, 185
Chandelier, 186-188
Character dolls, 46
Chintz, *See rooms*
Chisel, *See tools*
Christmas story, 46

Clay, 27
    Hands, 30, 53
    Heads, 28, 51
Clock — Instructions:
    Grandfather, 183
    Seth Thomas, 177
Clubs, women's, 38
Coal scuttle, *See rooms*
Collection — doll, 31, 37
Commercial doll, 46
Construction:
    Furniture, 129-194
    Pattern, *See plates*
    Rooms, 194-197
Cookery, 18
Corset, 1
Cost of dolls, 34
Costumes, *See patterns*
Cotton batting, *See patterns*
Counter sink, *See furniture*
Cradle, Colonial, 189
Creche figures, 146
Crinoline, *See basic patterns*
Crocheting — bedspread, 203
Crusade, 4
Cupboards, 200
Curls, 29

D

Damask, *See rooms*
Dental wax, 28
Display — dolls, 33, 44
Doctors, women, 8
Dolls:
    Can can, 125
    Character, 46
    Joseph, 46
    Mammy, 117
    Mermaid, 46
    Rag, 22
    Virgin Mary, 46
Door, 200
Draperies, *See rooms*
Drawers, *See furniture*

Drawing room, 194
Dresses, *See patterns*
Driftwood, 46
Drill, *See tools*
Dust ruffles, 203

E

Editor, 2
Editorials, 18
Education — women, 2, 4, 8
Eldridge, Charlotte, Chaps. 1-6
Emancipation, women's, 2, 4, 8
Emerson, 9
Engravings, steel, 10
Eyes, 28
Eyebrows, 28
Eyelashes, 28
Exhibit — dolls, 33, 44

F

Fabrics, 33, 36
Fabric sculptor, 36
Faces — dolls, 28, 51
Fairy tale dolls, 46
Fascia board, *See rooms*
Fashion print — Godey's, 2, 10, 23
Father, 40, 42
Features:
    Modeling, 51
    Painting, 52
Feet, 22
Female, 4
Female education, 4, 8
Fingers, 53
Finishes:
    Oil stain, 176
    Paint, 176
    Shellac, 176
    Varnish, 176
Fireplace, 194
Floor, setting, *See furniture*
Furniture, *See plates*
Furs, *See accessories*

G

Gauge, *See furniture*
Girl doll, 104
Gloves, *See accessories*
Glue, *See furniture*
Godey's Lady's Book, 4, 9, 10, 11, 18, 20, 22, 23, 38, 39
Godey Lady Doll, 20, 21, 24, 32
Godey, Louis Antoine, 2, 9, 10
Greeley, Horace, 9

H

Hair, doll's, 28, 29, 52
Hale, David, 2, 3
Hale, Sarah Josepha, 1, 2, 3, 8, 18, 38, 39
Hammer, *See tools*
Hands, doll's, 30, 53
Harp, French Empire, 188
Hats, *See patterns*
Hawthorne, Nathaniel, 9
Heads:
    Casting, 51
    Clay, 51
    Modeling, 51
    Papier mache, 51
    Plasticine, 28, 51
    Rag doll, 22
Headdresses, *See patterns*
Highboy, Early American, 191
Holmes, Oliver Wendell, 9
Hughes, Alice, 34
Husband, 28, 33, 35, 38, 41

I

Inspiration, 23
Interior decoration, 17

J

Jacket, *See patterns*
Jennings, Frances — Certificate, 34
Jewelry, *See patterns*
Joseph doll, 46

K

Kerchief, *See patterns*
Keyboard, piano, 181
Keys, piano, 181
Knife, *See tools*

L

Labor law, child, 8
Lacing, waist, 1
Ladies Magazine, 2
Lectures, 37-39
Legs, doll's, 22
Level, *See tools*
Literature, 9
Living room, 194
Longfellow, 9
Lumber, 176
Lyre, 46

M

Maline, 46
Manoreld, 45
Mantel, 198
Marbelized, tile, *See rooms*
Masculine public, 4
Masons, 3
Melodeon, 181
Mermaid, 46
Mitre, *See furniture*
Mitts, *See patterns*
Molds, doll's face, 51
Mortice, *See furniture*
Mother, 24, 32
Music rack, 182
Music room, 197

N

Nails, *See tools*
Newspaper publicity, 38, 39
Nippers, *See tools*
Northwood — novel, 3

O

Ohio, 48
Oil paint, 52

Oil stains, 176
Oil stone, *See tools*

P

Padding, *See patterns*
Paint: *See finishes*
 Oil, 176
 Shellac, 176
 Varnish, 176
Painting:
 Face, 52
 Hands, 53
Panel, *See patterns*
Panniers, *See patterns*
Pantalettes, *See basic patterns*
Papier mache, 28, 29
Parasol, *See patterns*
Paris, 9
Patterns:
 Basic, 57
 Body, 22, 51
 Doll, 51
 Dresses, 57-125
 Furniture, 130, 175-193
 Lingerie, 57
 Rooms, 194-198
 Shoes, 58
 Slippers, 58
Penwiper, butterfly, 17
Petticoat, *See basic patterns*
Piano, spinet, 181
Piano stool, 178
Pikelets, 18
Pilgrimage, 45
Pin cushion, lute, 17
Plans, house, 17
Plaster of Paris, 51
Plastic wood, *See furniture*
Plasticine clay, 27
Pleats, *See patterns*
Pliers, *See tools*
Plush, *See furniture*
Plywood, *See furniture*
Pneumonia, 3

Poe, Edgar Allan, 9
Price, Godey's Lady's Book, 20
Promoter, 10
Public, masculine, 4
Publisher, Louis Godey, Introduction

R

Rack, music, 182
Rag doll, 22
Rasp, *See tools*
Recipes, 18
Religious dolls, 46
Reticule, *See accessories*
Rockers, 178
Rooms, *See settings*
Rosettes, *See furniture*
Rugs, *See rooms*

S

Sandpaper, *See tools*
Satin, *See patterns*
Saw, *See tools*
Schoolmarm, 2
Screwdriver, *See tools*
Secretary, Early American, 192
Settings:
 Bedroom, 196, 197
 Living room, 194
 Music room, 197
Shaft, *See furniture*
Shawl, *See accessories*
Skating dress, 73
Sleeve, bell, 11
Sloanes, W. & J., 34
Sofa, rose back, 182, 183
Spinning wheel, 184
Stand, high wall back, 186
Steel engravings, 10
Stephanie, 22, 27, 35
Stop, drawer, *See furniture*
Stowe, Harriet Beecher, 9

T

Table, *See rooms*
Taffeta, *See dress patterns*

Television, 46, 48
Template, *See furniture*
Tenon, *See furniture*
Thanksgiving, 18
Tile, *See rooms*
Tin, 28
Tinted prints, 10
Tools, 175
Treadle, 185

U

Ulcer, 21-24, 27
Upholstering, *See furniture*

V

Vapors, 1
Varnish, *See finishes*
Vassar College, 4
Vassar, Matthew, 4
'Veneer, *See furniture*
Velvet, *See dress patterns*
Virgin Mary doll, 46

Volumes, bound, 20

W

Wainscot, 200
Wallboard, *See rooms*
Wall paper, *See rooms*
Wall stand, Colonial high back, 186
Warping, *See furniture*
Wash stand, 190
Washing machine, 8
Wax, 28
Whittier, 9
Whittling, *See furniture*
Window, 202
Window display, 33
Wine pudding, 18
Witch, 38
Women doctors, 8
Women, status of, 2, 4, 8
Wood filler, *See furniture*
Wrest pin, *See furniture*
Writing, 45